English for NSW YEAR 9

– STAGE 5 –

Emma Wynne-Jones
Bronwyn Ralphs

First published in 2023

Insight Publications Pty Ltd
3/350 Charman Road
Cheltenham Victoria 3192
Australia

Tel: +61 3 8571 4950
Fax: +61 3 8571 0257
Email: books@insightpublications.com.au

www.insightpublications.com.au

A catalogue record for this book is available from the National Library of Australia

English for NSW, Year 9, Stage 5 / Emma Wynne-Jones, Bronwyn Ralphs

ISBN:

9781923016255

Edited by Hannah Cartmel

Cover by Melisa Paredes

Internal design by Federico Fonseca

Typesetting by Sardine

Printed by Markono Print Media Pte Ltd

CONTENTS

CONTENTS

UNIT 01

Around the world

Unit inquiry question:
How do texts from different parts of the world reflect and shape our understanding of people, cultures and global interconnectedness?

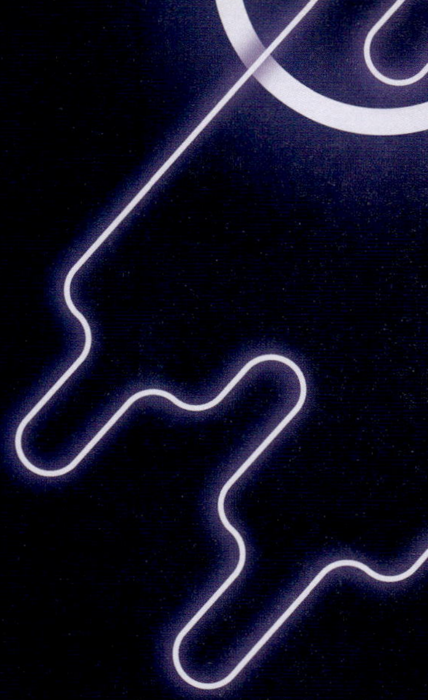

In this unit, students will think critically about the ways in which texts from around the world can broaden perspectives and deepen our understanding of other people, communities and cultures. The unit also invites students to consider the role of literature in fostering a sense of global interconnectedness.

This unit has been broken into three chapters, each of which looks at a different aspect of texts and the world and raises additional inquiry questions.

By exploring the inquiry question across the three chapters, students can develop a comprehensive and nuanced understanding of how texts can reflect and contribute to our understanding of global diversity. Students will analyse how texts use language to reflect values and shape perspectives on tradition, diversity and opportunity.

CHAPTER 1

The land down under

Students will explore a variety of texts to reflect upon what it means to be Australian in a culturally diverse society.

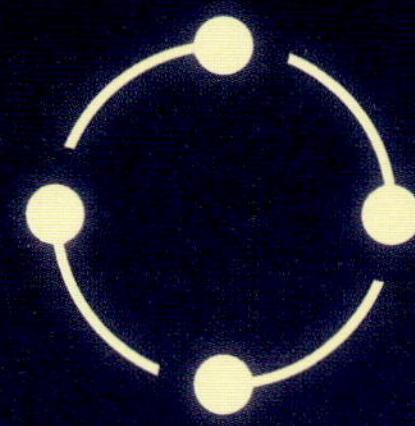

CHAPTER 2

The land of opportunity

Students will examine American literature and consider how it is reflective of American culture.

CHAPTER 3

The land of contradiction

Students will consider how literature can represent conflicting perspectives on the same individual and how this shapes perceptions and values.

The learning activities within each chapter and the summative assessment options (on page 45) provide opportunities to assess student achievement of the following outcomes:

Outcome and Focus Area	Content point
EN5-RVL-01 Reading, viewing and listening to texts	**Reading for challenge, interest and enjoyment**
	Read increasingly complex texts that challenge thinking, pique interest, enhance enjoyment and provoke a personal response Consider how the social, cultural and ethical positions represented in texts represent, affirm or challenge views of the world
	Reflecting
	Reflect on how reading promotes a broad and balanced understanding of the world and enables students to explore wider universal issues
EN5-URA-01 Understanding and responding to texts A	**Connotation, imagery and symbol**
	Analyse how figurative language and devices can be used to represent complex ideas, thoughts and feelings to contribute to larger patterns of meaning in texts, and experiment with this in own texts
EN5-URB-01 Understanding and responding to texts B	**Perspective and context**
	Analyse how texts can be understood or interpreted from different perspectives, and experiment with this idea in own texts Explain how texts affirm or challenge established cultural attitudes and values in different contexts
EN5-ECA-01 Expressing ideas and composing texts A	**Writing**
	Develop a personal and informed voice that generate ideas and position an audience through selection of appropriate word-level language and text-level features
	Text features
	Express ideas, using appropriate structures for purpose and audience, that reflect an emerging personal style
	Sentence-level grammar and punctuation
	Craft concise sentences to suit text purpose
	Word-level language
	Select technical vocabulary to write with accuracy in a range of modes and registers appropriate to audience, purpose, form and context
EN5-ECB-01 Expressing ideas and composing texts B	**Planning, monitoring and revising**
	Research, summarise, evaluate and synthesise information and perspectives from different sources to generate new ideas and create detailed and informed texts

CHAPTER 1: THE LAND DOWN UNDER

Chapter overview

In this chapter you will explore a variety of texts that reflect upon what it means to be Australian in a culturally diverse society.

You will consider different ideas about what being Australian is for different people and how these perspectives are conveyed through different texts.

Success criteria: In this chapter, I will be successful when I can …

- recognise different perspectives in texts
- use key words and ideas to explore the topic of cultural diversity
- examine how texts can have different interpretations
- evaluate how figurative language is used to convey complex ideas and feelings
- convey my ideas creatively and critically in my writing
- reflect on how my understanding of the world has been broadened.

Chapter inquiry questions

- What does it mean to be 'Australian'?
- What does it mean to live in a culturally diverse community?
- How can we recognise and appreciate diverse perspectives and experiences?

Key vocabulary

- Culture
- Diversity
- Discrimination
- Representation

What does it mean to be 'Australian'?

We all have different experiences of living in Australia, and these experiences influence our understanding of what it means to live in this country. Multiculturism has developed over the years with many people from many countries making Australia the place they call home. In unique ways, everyone can feel proud to be Australian and celebrate different characteristics of being Australian.

1.1.1 Warm-up

Writing challenge

These three simple sentences don't flow well:
The lamington was made of sponge cake. It was covered in coconut. It was yummy.

Improve them.

Tips: Use connectives to join these simple sentences together. You could try to create a question and an exclamation. Use sensory imagery to make your reader's mouth water.

1.1.2 Reading, viewing and listening to texts

Look at this image:

1 Write a sentence explaining the purpose of this visual text.

2 A perspective is a point of view, and different texts can offer varying perspectives. Look at the poster – what perspective is this poster offering about what it is to be Australian?

3 Do you agree with this perspective? Justify your answer.

4 In considering this poster, your perspective of the topic of Australian identity might be influenced by your age, gender, ethnicity or culture. Choose a different perspective to explore, using these sentence-starters:

I am thinking of ... [the topic] from the viewpoint of ... [the viewpoint you've chosen].
I think ... [describe the topic from your viewpoint].

Be an actor – take on the character of your viewpoint.

1.1.3 Understanding and responding to texts A and B

Language has the power to both reflect and shape individual and collective identity.

1 What 'identity' do you think is being reflected and shaped in the poster?

2 How do you think the visual features are being used as symbols?

3 Discuss with a partner if this identity is similar to how you see your own? Why/why not?

What does it mean to live in a culturally diverse community?

Some Australians see the benefits of living in a culturally diverse community.

'Australia is a land where you are free to be whoever you want to be, whatever you want to do and however you want to do it. No one judges you by your position or title; you are respected for the person you are and not by your job or how much money you have. You have the freedom to travel, meet interesting people from all around the world and discover different places and different cultures all in one country.' (Jenish Pandya, 'What does being an Australian mean to you?' by Harita Mehta, *SBS Hindi, 25 January 2018)*

Is this perspective true to your experience?

PAUSE AND CONSIDER: Before reading the following extract, find out more about racism in Australia through the Australian Human Rights Commission. Visit their website and read about the 'Racism. It Stops With Me' campaign, then talk with a small group about what you have learned.

Let's explore some attitudes towards cultural diversity by reading an extract from Maxine Beneba Clarke's memoir, *The Hate Race*. This memoir reads like a narrative and tells the story of the author, whose parents migrated to Australia in the early 1970s, and her experience as the target of racist remarks and encounters.

1.1.4 Reading, viewing and listening to texts

The Hate Race

By Maxine Beneba Clarke

What different meanings are associated with the words in the title? Brainstorm some ideas around the title.

'Where are you from?' my teacher asked brightly.

'Pardon, Mrs Kingsley?'

'Where are you from?'

Unsure of the answer she wanted, I stared at her for a moment.

What is the **tone** of the teacher when she asks the question 'Where are you from?' at the beginning of this extract? Circle the words that you think convey the teacher's tone.

'From my mum's tummy,' I replied matter-of-factly.

A faint titter of amusement ran around the room. The class was suddenly extremely attentive.

'That's not what I meant, Maxine,' said my teacher curtly.

I stared at her, confused.

'The class is interested in where you're from, Maxine,' she said insistently.

I racked my brain, staring at the clear plastic boxes of counting blocks stacked up on the bookshelf behind Mrs Kingsley. I imagined myself tipping them all out, fashioning them into a Lego-like ladder and climbing away out of the classroom window.

'From my mum's ... vagina?' I said **tentatively**.

The class erupted into giggles.

'You rude girl!' Mrs Kingsley looked furious. 'You know what I am asking. Why are you being so **insolent**? What country were you born in?'

VOCABULARY

Tentative
adverb: to do something in a hesitant or uncertain way.

Insolent
adjective: boldly rude or disrespectful.

'This one.' My head was hurting now.

'Oh,' said Mrs Kingsley 'Well ... where are your parents from?'

'They came here from England.'

Mrs Kingsley was glaring at me again. A boy called Matthew, who was sitting at the back of the room, right next to where our teacher was standing, started laughing.

'They're not from England!' he said scathingly. 'My nanna's from England and your parents are not like her. They're not English, Mrs Kingsley!'

Discuss what you think Maxine is feeling at this point.

I knew my parents had come to Australia from England. I had even been back there when I was smaller, to visit my grandparents and cousins. I remembered a bit of it. There were photos of me and Cecelia and Bronson on a sled in the snow with our gumboots and parkas on.

'I want you to go home and ask your parents where they're from,' said my teacher. 'And you can come back and tell us properly tomorrow. Does anyone have any other questions?'

Rebecca, a sweet pale-faced girl with red hair, raised her arm.

'Yes, Rebecca?' My teacher seemed relieved that the conversation was moving along.

'What do ... people like you ... feel like?'

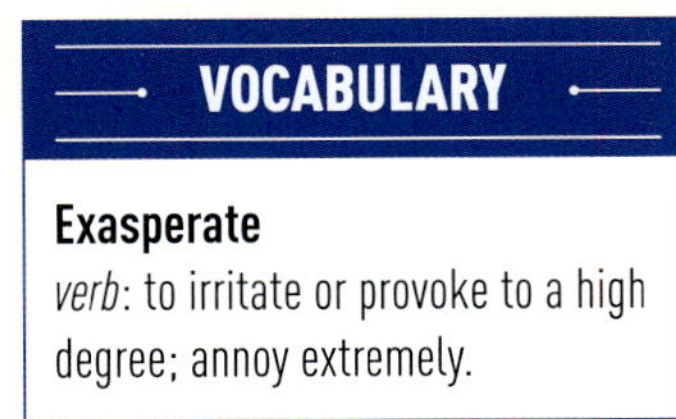

Discuss what you think the description of the setting adds to the scene.

'What do you mean, Rebecca?' Mrs Kingsley asked, **exasperated**.

'You'll have to explain the question to her a little better than that, darling.'

'I mean, do you have normal feelings ... like normal people do?'

Silence fell over the classroom as all of the other six-year-olds waited eagerly for my answer. Outside the classroom window, a pack of galahs was tearing apart one of the gum trees, shrieking and squawking as they tore the nuts from the branches and dropped them onto the wooden seats below. I looked over at them for a moment, then back into the classroom. The three ceiling fans hummed as they whirred lopsidedly around.

'I don't know,' I said quietly. 'I don't know if I have normal feelings like normal people do.'

When my Student of the Week question time had finished, Mrs Kingsley asked me to choose a piece of A4 cardboard to use for my Student of the Week album. I chose a sunflower-yellow piece of card, and walked slowly back to my seat. The cardboard would be passed around the class that day, with each student writing down something nice about me in brightly coloured pencil. At the end of the day, the poster would be pinned to the noticeboard, and at the end of the week, I'd get to take it home. I watched, throughout the day, as the brightly coloured rectangle moved from desk to desk. Eventually, it landed on the desk next to mine. My best friend Jennifer slowly read down the page, looked over at me, picked up her pink pencil and began to write. She worked away for about ten minutes, stopping every now and then to think.

Jennifer was a shy girl with thin brown-blonde hair and a delicate sparrow-like face. Her family, the McGuires, had been one of the few that had welcomed my parents on their arrival in Kellyville, and us kids were frequently at their house playing with Jen and her brother and sister.

Jen had been at preschool with me, and we started school at the same time. We never spoke about the differences between us, or about the indignities I suffered on account of them, but in my memories of early primary school Jen is always there, standing next to me, unmoving.

'Once you've finished, hand the album over to Maxine, please, dear,' Mrs Kingsley instructed.

'Then she can read it out and we can pin it up.'

Reluctantly, Jennifer handed me the piece of card. I ran my eyes down the misspelled comments.

Maxine is brown.
Maxine has brown skin.
Maxine has funny curly hair.
Maxine thinks her family is from England.
Maxine has dark brown skin.
Maxine is nice and Maxine is black.
Maxine is friendly.
Maxine is not Australian.
Maxine is brown and she does dancing.
Maxine has a black family and a little brother.

Maxine doesn't know about her feelings.
Maxine is brown.
She is brown.
She has brown skin.

At the bottom of the list was a whole paragraph written neatly in bright pink pencil.

'Stand up and read out your album, Maxine!' Mrs Kingsley said. 'I'm sure the class had some lovely things to write about you.'

I stood up, pushing my chair back away from the desk, and read out the one pink paragraph at the bottom, written by my friend Jennifer.

'Maxine is friendly and smart. She is a good reader. She plays the piano. She has a brother and a sister. She is very good at spelling. She is a happy girl, and I like to play with her. She is my friend.'

What do you think Maxine is feeling as she reads this long list of comments?

1.1.5 Understanding and responding to texts A and B

1 What does the colour of Maxine's skin symbolise in this extract? Discuss with a partner.

2 Maxine is confronted by different perspectives towards cultural diversity in the extract. Complete the table below to show your understanding.

What's their view?	What's your evidence?
The teacher	
The other students in Maxine's class	
Her best friend	

1.1.6 Expressing ideas and composing texts A Extension activity

Let's return to the earlier quotation: 'Australia is a land where you are free to be whoever you want to be, whatever you want to do and however you want to do it.'

Does this statement reflect the **cultural perspective** shown in the extract? Justify your response with reference to the extract.

VOCABULARY

Cultural perspective
noun: a cultural perspective is how individuals are shaped by their environments as well as social and cultural factors such as nationality, race and gender.

How can we recognise and appreciate diverse perspectives and experiences?

Recognising and appreciating diverse perspectives and experiences is important as it allows us to gain a broader understanding of the world around us. Reading and viewing texts helps us to appreciate how crucial this is if we want to create a more tolerant, inclusive and respectful society.

1.1.7 Reading, viewing and listening to texts

Search online or scan the QR code, for the article titled 'Children's books must be diverse, or kids will grow up believing white is superior', published on *The Conversation* website.

Scan the QR code.

1 Read the article from *The Conversation* about how important books are for children growing up to recognise and understand the diversity in our Australian society.
Complete the Think-Pair-Share activity:

THINK What perspectives about reading diverse stories are given in the story? Do you agree with the views offered?	**PAIR**	**SHARE** Have you identified the same things from the article? Share your opinions about the ideas offered.

2 Complete the vocabulary finder:

Word to define	Your definition	Use the word in a sentence to show how it would be used
Bias		
Stereotype		
Prejudice		
Reconciliation		

1.1.8 Expressing ideas and composing texts A

1 Write a paragraph agreeing or disagreeing with the following statement. Use examples from any of the texts in the chapter, and your own lived experience to justify your response.

'Children need everyday story books with heroes and characters that reflect their diverse backgrounds.'

2 How do people's experiences and backgrounds shape their perspectives on the world?

1.1.9 Expressing ideas and composing texts A and B 

Activity A: Creative collage

Create a collage. Collect a range of images (both art and media sources) that depict characters that you perceive as 'typically Australian'. Once finished, reflect on the following questions:

1 What 'typically Australian' qualities do we associate with these characters?
2 Are these qualities seen as positive? Why/why not?
3 Do these qualities reflect the reality of what it means to be Australian?
4 Explain how these images might have influenced perceptions of Australian identity.

Activity B: Imaginative writing

Select one of the images from your collage to create an imaginative piece of writing, with a focus on developing character. Your challenge is to create a character that has an authentic Australian identity, so it will a good idea to plan and draft your work before you decide on a final response.

Begin your response with this sentence from *The Hate Race*: 'Where are you from?'

How is cultural diversity reflected in texts, and does this ever differ from lived experiences? Discuss as a class.

1.1.10 Chapter reflection

Our perspectives and experiences of cultural diversity are varied. Our perspectives are often dependent on our personal context and experiences. The texts we have looked at use imagery, figurative language and punctuation to convey these viewpoints and engage readers.

Summarise the perspectives of cultural diversity shown in the three texts presented in this chapter.

Text	What perspective does the composer present about cultural diversity? What does the composer want us to appreciate about cultural diversity?
'Man your eskies' poster	
The Hate Race by Maxine Beneba Clarke	
'Children's books must be diverse ...' from *The Conversation*	

1 Now, reflect on your own experience. Have your experiences of cultural diversity been similar or different to these?

2 Let's return to the unit inquiry question: ***How do texts from different parts of the world reflect and shape our understanding of people, cultures and global interconnectedness?*** How have these three texts broadened or challenged your understanding of cultural diversity?

CHAPTER 2

THE LAND OF OPPORTUNITY

Chapter overview

In this chapter you will read texts by American writers. The United States (US) is often called the 'land of opportunity' and you can explore notions of American culture and how these are represented in a variety of texts and videos. You can reflect on how people's experiences and backgrounds can shape their perspectives on their world.

Success criteria: In this chapter, I will be successful when I can ...

- recognise that people have different experiences depending on their social context
- understand how the voice in a text can create meaning for the reader
- reflect on how writers convey adversity and success
- convey my ideas creatively and critically in my writing.

Chapter inquiry questions

- How can a text convey an impression of a culture?
- How do people's experiences and backgrounds shape their perspective on the world?
- In the face of adversity, why do some individuals prevail and others fail?

Key vocabulary

- Voice
- Context
- Opportunity

How can a text convey an impression of a culture?

A phrase you might have heard connected to American culture is the 'American Dream'. This phrase was coined in 1931 by writer and historian James Truslow Adams. He described it as the 'dream of a land in which life should be better and richer and fuller for everyone'. The 'American Dream' is the belief that anyone can achieve success in life through hard work, sacrifice and taking risks.

1.2.1 Warm-up with a partner!

Think	Pair	Share
What might the American Dream look like for you?	Join with a friend and discuss your ideas – write down what their dream is.	What do you think is needed to make your dream come true?

1.2.2 Reading, viewing and listening to texts

Read the poem below, written by Gwendolyn Brooks in 1959.

Watch the video below as this will give you an insightful visual representation of the poem and help to deepen your understanding.

Scan the QR code or research online to watch the video.

We Real Cool

The pool players.
Seven at the golden shovel.

By Gwendolyn Brooks

We real cool. We
Left school. We

Lurk late. We
Strike straight. We

Sing sin. We
Thin gin. We

Jazz June. We
Die soon.

1 Discuss with a partner in what ways did listening to and watching the visual representation of the poem help you form an impression of American culture?

2 Does this support or contradict your view of American culture?

1.2.3 Understanding and responding to texts A

1 How would you describe the rhythm created in this poem?

2 Brooks has used a variety of different stylistic features to help create such a rhythm – find the evidence from the poem and complete the table below.

Remember to use quotation marks!

Poetic technique	Best evidence
rhyme	
alliteration	
punctuation	
repetition	

3 What is the stylistic impact of the repetition of 'We' at the end of the line? Why do you think Brooks has structured her poem like this?

4 In this poem, whose voice does the reader hear? What is the tone [of voice] created in the poem?

VOCABULARY

Voice
noun: communicates what the narrator's thinks or believes through how the author makes word choices to describe feelings, characters, events.

5 What impression of the 'American Dream' is the reader given in this poem?

How do people's experiences and backgrounds shape their perspective on the world?

All writers are influenced by the context in which they live. When we, as readers, make meaning from their words we also interpret them within our own experiences. It is our experiences that shape our perspectives on our world, both as writers and readers.

1.2.4 Reading, viewing and listening to texts

Read the short extract below written by Chinese American author Amy Tan. Tan was born in the US of Chinese immigrant parents, and her stories often explore the tensions between her parents' traditional Chinese background and experience and her desire to be an 'ordinary' American girl.

Fish cheeks

By Amy Tan

Highlight the phrases that show the reader the narrator is conflicted about her Chinese background.

I fell in love with the minister's son the winter I turned fourteen. He was not Chinese, but as white as Mary in the manger. For Christmas I prayed for this blond-haired boy, Robert, and a slim new American nose.

When I found out that my parents had invited the minister's family over for Christmas Eve dinner, I cried. What would Robert think of our shabby Chinese Christmas? What would he think of our noisy Chinese relatives who lacked proper American manners? What terrible disappointment would he feel upon seeing not a roasted turkey and sweet potatoes but Chinese food?

On Christmas Eve I saw that my mother had outdone herself in creating a strange menu. She was pulling black veins out of the backs of fleshy prawns. The kitchen was littered with **appalling** mounds of raw food: A slimy rock cod with bulging eyes that pleaded not to be thrown into a pan of hot oil. Tofu, which looked like stacked wedges of rubbery white sponges. A bowl soaking dried fungus back to life. A plate of squid, their backs crisscrossed with knife markings so they resembled bicycle tires.

And then they arrived – the minister's family and all my relatives in a **clamor** of doorbells and rumpled Christmas packages. Robert grunted hello, and I pretended he was not worthy of existence.

Dinner threw me deeper into despair. My relatives licked the ends of their chopsticks and reached across the table, dipping them into the dozen or so plates of food. Robert and his family waited patiently for platters to be passed to them. My relatives murmured with pleasure when my mother brought out the whole steamed fish. Robert **grimaced**. Then my father poked his chopsticks just below the fish eye and plucked out the soft meat. 'Amy, your favorite,' he said, offering me the tender fish cheek. I wanted to disappear.

At the end of the meal my father leaned back and belched loudly, thanking my mother for her fine cooking. 'It's a polite Chinese custom to show you are satisfied,' explained my father to our astonished guests. Robert was looking down at his plate with a reddened face. The minister managed to muster up a quiet burp. I was stunned into silence for the rest of the night.

After everyone had gone, my mother said to me, 'You want to be the same as American girls on the outside.' She handed me an early gift. It was a miniskirt in beige tweed. 'But inside you must always be Chinese. You must be proud you are different. Your only shame is to have shame.'

And even though I didn't agree with her then, I knew that she understood how much I had suffered during the evening's dinner. It wasn't until many years later – long after I had gotten over my crush on Robert – that I was able to fully appreciate her lesson and the true purpose behind our particular menu. For Christmas Eve that year, she had chosen all my favorite foods.

VOCABULARY

Appalling
adjective: causing shock, disgust or alarm.

Clamor [US], clamour [AUS]
noun: a loud and confusing noise.

In two different colours highlight the DESCRIPTIVE words/phrases that show the difference between the narrator's family and Robert's family.

VOCABULARY

Grimace
verb: to show disapproval in your facial expression.

Read the highlighted paragraph carefully and discuss it with a partner. What do you think the narrator's mother is telling her about the importance of background and experience?

1.2.5 Understanding and responding to texts A and B

1 In this extract, Amy Tan is embarrassed by her Chinese heritage. What was her 'American Dream' this particular Christmas?

2 Research online a little bit more about Amy Tan and decide whether or not she has realised the 'American Dream' – justify your answer.

3 Re-read paragraph two. What rhetorical technique does Tan use to develop the narrator's voice and reveal her feelings about her mother's invitation?

4 Look carefully at the words used to describe her family, and in contrast Robert's family. Complete the table below:

Words to describe Tan's family	Words to describe Robert's family

5 What is the effect of the contrast in Tan's word choices here?

Extension activity

What might be the positive and negative consequences of ignoring your family's background culture in favour of something more popular or 'normal'?

1.2.6 Expressing ideas and composing texts A

At the end of the story, Tan's mother gives her some advice which she doesn't understand until she is much older. Write about a time when an adult has offered you or someone you know advice which was ignored.

1. What was the advice? Who gave it?
2. Why was it ignored?
3. What were the consequences of not heeding the advice?
4. On reflection, do you think the right decision was made? Justify your thinking.

In the face of adversity, why do some individuals prevail and others fail?

The 'American Dream' is a concept that is explored in many works of American literature, but it can also be clearly seen in the way that the notion of celebrity is seen in our society. In American culture, as well as Australian, sports celebrities are prominent. However, it is easy to embark on a dream of sporting accolades and fame, but very few truly achieve greatness.

DISCUSS

What does it take to be a success?
What makes some individuals succeed when others do not?
What does success look like for you?

1.2.7 Reading, viewing and listening to texts

Read the following abridged article about the success of NBA player Kobe Bryant and complete the activities below.

Scan the QR code or research online to read the full article.

How Kobe Bryant willed himself to greatness

By Colin Robertson, 4 October 2015

When he was 12 years old, Kobe Bryant was about to give up basketball forever. He just completed his summer basketball camp and was going home a disgrace.

He thought it would be the beginning of a flawless journey to becoming the star NBA player that we all know today – especially because his father, Joe Bryant, played in the NBA for 8 years before playing his final 6 years in Italy ...

He entered the camp and played against some of the most talented youngsters in the country – and they embarrassed him. Bryant did not score a single point. Not one jumper, not one layup, not even one free throw. Nothing.

THE TURNING POINT

He spent that entire summer in frustration – questioning whether basketball was really for him ... so why dream of becoming a basketball player when he clearly had no talent for it?

Then Kobe read about one of his heroes, Michael Jordan. He learned how Michael got cut from his high school basketball team, but didn't quit.

When Kobe learned this, a fire was created inside of him that would never be put out.

THE WILL OF KOBE BRYANT

When Kobe entered high school, he got to the gym every day at 5am and would not leave the afternoon practice until 7pm!

After the official practice was over, he convinced his teammates to play one-on-one games with him up to 100 points.

He singled out any player that could help him improve his skills and forced them to challenge him.

This relentless work ethic over his high school career turned him into one of the best players in the country. So good, in fact, that just 6 years after he failed to score a single point in basketball camp, Kobe was drafted 13th overall in the NBA.

But his work ethic didn't stop there. He pushed himself even harder as an NBA player.

He practiced by himself, sometimes even without a ball, hours before his teammates showed up to the gym.

He forced himself to make 400 shots every single practice. He put himself through 4 hours of intense workouts on game days!

He completely cut out sugar and had one of the strictest diets in the NBA ...

PROOF THAT SUCCESS IS IN YOUR CONTROL

This proves that if someone followed Kobe Bryant's path, he could reach the same level of success.

There is nothing preventing another boy entering his first year of high school from getting to the gym at 5am and practicing until 7pm.

There is nothing stopping him from recognizing areas of weakness in his game and working relentlessly to improve them.

There is nothing stopping him from following a strict diet, or doing intense 4-hour workouts on game days.

Nor is there anything stopping him from meticulously counting 400 made shots every single day.

All of these practices are within the control of anyone. Which means achieving the level of success of Kobe Bryant is also within the control of anyone!

So why aren't more people as successful as Kobe Bryant?

Because following his path is hard, painful, and boring. It requires something more than simply knowing what to do. It requires ... willpower.

HOW TO DEVELOP KOBE BRYANT'S WILLPOWER

Unlike almost everything else in life, your willpower is something that you have complete control over. You cannot control your circumstances, your luck, or other people in your life.

But you can control your decisions and your actions.

Let's unpack Kobe's story to see how he was able to develop the willpower to become one of the greatest basketball players of all time.

1. FIND A HERO

Heroes have the ability to inspire you in ways you may not think ...

If someone told 12 year-old Kobe that he could become a great basketball player if he just 'outworks everyone' it would not have inspired him in the same way.

But because he read the story about Michael Jordan, he could see himself in Michael's shoes ...

2. MAKE SACRIFICES

'There's a choice that we have to make as people ... What I mean by that is the inherent sacrifices that come along with that. Being a great friend, son, nephew, there are sacrifices that come along with making that choice.' – Kobe Bryant

Kobe achieved greatness because ... he understood that he had to make sacrifices to reach that goal.

3. BE RELENTLESS

In his last year of high school, Kobe Bryant was unquestionably the best player in the country. This could have made him arrogant ...

When he got to the NBA, he worked even harder ...

Even today ... he is still fighting. Because Kobe knows that greatness is about always doing your best. No matter what.

CONCLUSION

Kobe Bryant is living proof that achieving greatness does not require talent, circumstances, or luck. It requires a desire to be the best you possibly can and a will to do whatever it takes to get there.

It all started by becoming inspired by a hero, making sacrifices for what he truly wanted, and relentlessly pursuing it for his entire career. After researching Kobe's story, I can genuinely say he is one of my greatest heroes. And an inspiration to anyone who is willing to do whatever it takes.

1.2.8 Understanding and responding to texts A and B

1 Identify three qualities that you think were instrumental in helping Kobe Bryant achieve his own American Dream.

1 ______________________________

2 ______________________________

3 ______________________________

2 What were the disadvantages of Bryant achieving his dream?

____

____

3 In the following table you will read some lines from the article that use stylistic features to engage the audience and encourage them to connect with Bryant's story. Discuss each one with a partner, try to identify a language technique and how it creates this connection.

Notice that you are drawing on your knowledge of literary techniques as you analyse this non-fiction article.

A clue has been bolded in some of the quotations to help you.

Quotation	Stylistic feature/technique	Effect?
'Bryant did not score a single point. **Not one** jumper, **not one** layup, not even one free throw. Nothing.'	The repetition of the same phrase in a sentence is called ANAPHORA. In this example 'not one' is anaphora.	The use of anaphora emphasises to the reader that when Bryant first started basketball he exhibited no obvious talent, which makes his rise to success even more amazing.
'so why dream of becoming a basketball player when he clearly had no talent for it**?**'		
'Because following his path is **hard, painful, and boring**.'		
'he could see himself in **Michael's shoes**.'		

In the conclusion, this article states that, 'Kobe Bryant is living proof that achieving greatness does not require talent, circumstances, or luck. It requires a desire to be the best you possibly can and a will to do whatever it takes to get there.'

4 **Do you agree or disagree with this statement? Justify your point of view with examples from your own experiences.**

1.2.9 Expressing ideas and composing texts A

Write a short imaginative piece using one of the following titles:

- My dream
- Challenge or opportunity?
- The chance of a lifetime

Is America truly 'the land of opportunity'? Discuss with a partner.

1.2.10 Chapter reflection

Our perspectives and experiences of culture are varied. Your perspectives are often dependent on your personal context and experiences. The texts we have looked at use imagery, figurative language and punctuation to convey these viewpoints and engage readers.
Summarise the perspectives of how cultural diversity can bring opportunity in the three texts presented in this chapter.

Text	What perspective does the composer present about the cultural diversity of America? What do the composers want us to appreciate or criticise about this 'land of opportunity'?
'We Real Cool' by Gwendoline Brooks	
'Fish cheeks' by Amy Tan	
'How Kobe Bryant willed himself to greatness' by Colin Robertson	

1 Have your experiences of cultural diversity and the opportunities offered in Australian culture been similar or different to these?

2 Let's return to the unit inquiry question: ***How do texts from different parts of the world reflect and shape our understanding of people, cultures and global interconnectedness?*** How have these three texts broadened or challenged your understanding of being in a global society?

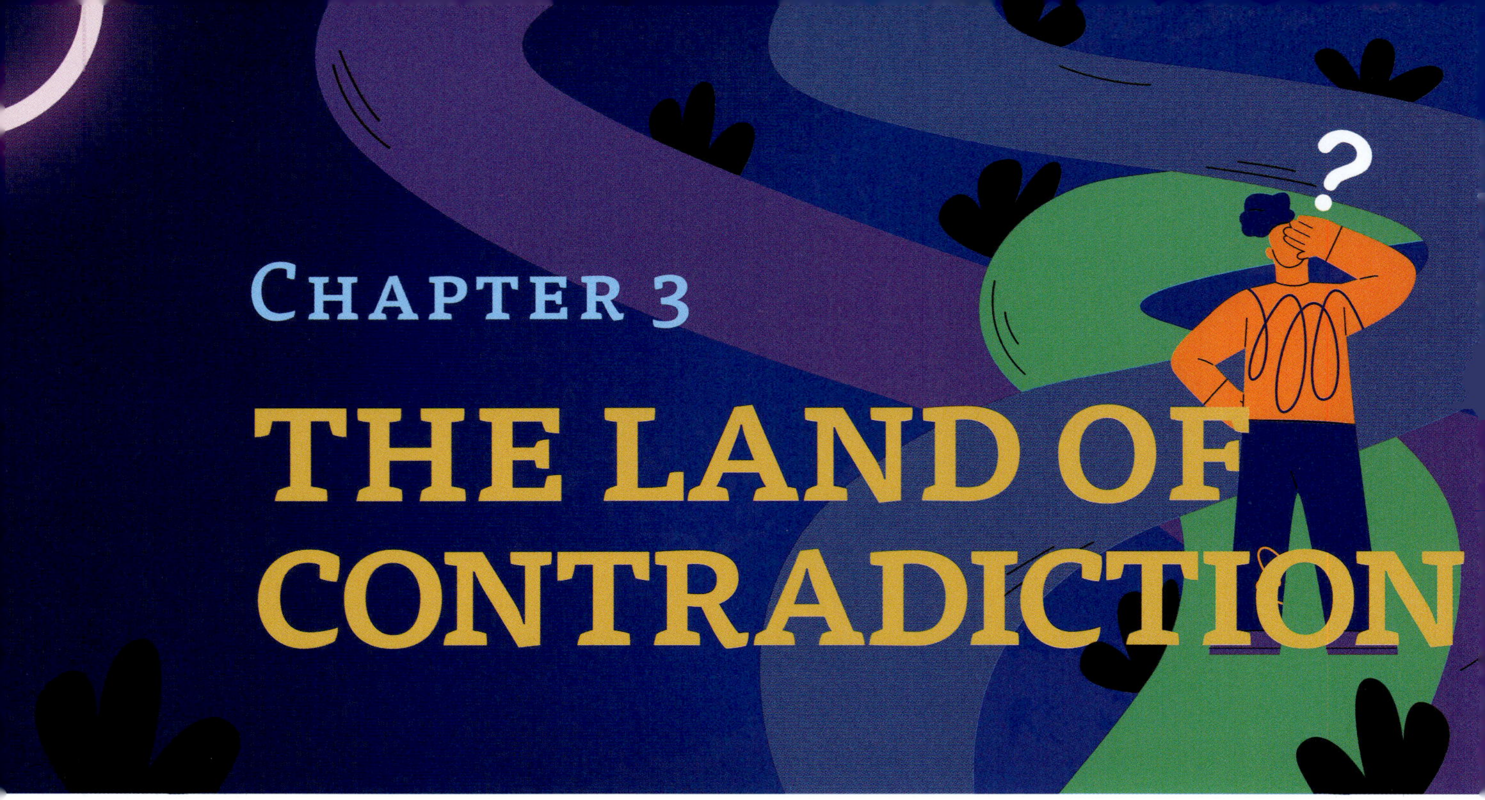

CHAPTER 3

THE LAND OF CONTRADICTION

Chapter overview

In this chapter, you will consider how texts reflect and shape particular perspectives of other people and how these perspectives can contradict. Living in our modern world, and being globally connected, is often like living in a land of contradictions. We need to navigate it carefully. In this land, you will come across points of view that disagree with each other, and the waters will be murky. To become critical thinkers and discerning readers and viewers, you must understand that very little is neutral.

You will explore the ways in which perspective influences our perceptions. By thinking about and examining how perspective shapes the way ideas are represented, you will be able to consider events, people and ideas from different points of view.

In your responding and composing, you will examine assumptions and underlying meanings, and the range of different meanings made possible with contradicting perspectives.

Success criteria: In this chapter, I will be successful when I can ...

- read, view and understand extracts from visual and print texts

Chapter inquiry questions

- How can we have contradictory perspectives?
- How do texts use language to shape our perspective?
- How do we interpret conflicting perspectives and deal with contradictions?

Key vocabulary

- Perspective
- Connotation
- Modality
- Gaze

- understand, identify and explain how contextual, creative and unconscious influences shape the composition, understanding and interpretation of representations
- analyse how texts can be understood or interpreted from different perspectives, and experiment with this idea in my texts
- research, evaluate and synthesise different perspectives to come up with my own ideas and compositions
- reflect on the challenges or complexities of contradictory perspectives.

How can we have contradictory perspectives?

We discussed a little about perspectives in Chapter 1. A perspective is created by the way we see things and the ideas we have when we read or write something. When we read, the writer's values and ideas are shown through the words they use and how they organise the text. This can make us agree or disagree with their ideas.

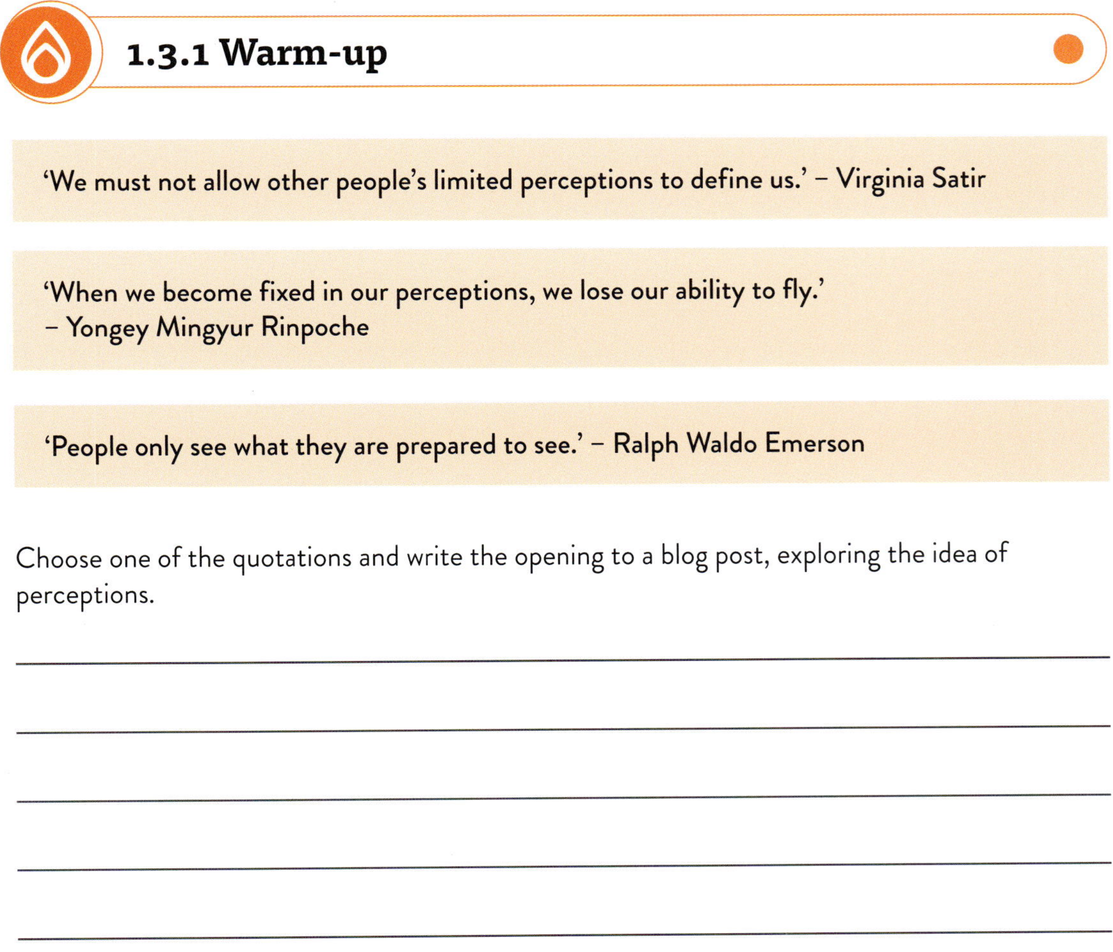

1.3.1 Warm-up

'We must not allow other people's limited perceptions to define us.' – Virginia Satir

'When we become fixed in our perceptions, we lose our ability to fly.'
– Yongey Mingyur Rinpoche

'People only see what they are prepared to see.' – Ralph Waldo Emerson

Choose one of the quotations and write the opening to a blog post, exploring the idea of perceptions.

By looking at things from different perspectives, we can discover underlying values in a text and different meanings that might change or support what the writer originally intended. It can also make us question the writer's ideas and our own, and perhaps change our thinking.

We all see the world differently because of our culture and beliefs. These perspectives shape the way we think and make us more likely to agree with certain ideas. It's important for us to realise how these perspectives affect our views so that we can decide whether we want to agree with those ideas or not.

1.3.2 Reading, viewing and listening to texts

1 To help illustrate this idea of perspective, look at this cartoon:

2 With a partner, discuss. Who is right? Who is wrong?

As you can see, for one person the number is 6 and for the other, it's the number 9. They are both right and wrong, depending on the perspective. The world is a complex place where observations from different perspectives can seem contradictory. If one person changes their position, they will understand the other's perspective. But, how can we have different perspectives?

You must shift your focus to see the other image. But once you know it's there you will always see both. This is what happens with perspective. For a period of time, you will only see things in a particular way and have only one view. However, once you are forced to see that there is a different way of seeing the same thing, you need to decide whether to accept or dismiss this new perspective.

To help illustrate this point, read the following poem by Brian Bilston.

Every day the planet burns a little more

By Brian Bilston

We only have a short while
So quick, let me tell you
We're too far gone to turn this around
I can't believe
We have it in us to put this world right
It is all too late, too late
How can you say
But do not give up hope

Every day the planet burns a little more
And hot air rises
While governments pump out empty promises
We are powerless
Don't be so foolish to imagine that
Together we have a voice
Big enough to change the world
The decisions we make each day are
Unimportant
The food we eat, the things we buy, how we get around
How naïve to think
The destruction of centuries could be undone
In a few decades
If we could just find reverse

(now read this poem from bottom to top)

3 Identify one aspect of the poetic structure that alters the reader's perspective.

____

4 How do you think this helps Bilston to communicate his message about perspective?

____

____

How do texts use language to shape our perspective?

> 'Why did they think that by killing him, he would cease to exist as a fighter? Today he is in every place, wherever there is a just cause to defend. His unerasable mark is now in history and his luminous gaze of a prophet has become a symbol for all the poor of this world.' – Fidel Castro

Texts have the power to shape how we see and understand people, groups, situations, events and ideas through language. In this section, we'll explore how texts specifically use language to present certain viewpoints about people and how these viewpoints can affect our own perspectives.

We are going to learn about one significant historical and influential figure who became a powerful symbol for revolutionary action: Che Guevara.

1.3.3 Reading, viewing and listening to texts

Ernesto 'Che' Guevara was a notable communist and leader in South America.

1 Read the following famous quotations by Che Guevara:

> 'If you tremble with indignation at every injustice, then you are a comrade of mine.'

> 'We cannot be sure of having something to live for unless we are willing to die for it.'

> 'The revolution is not an apple that falls when it is ripe. You have to make it fall.'

> 'The true revolutionary is guided by a great feeling of love. It is impossible to think of a genuine revolutionary lacking this quality.'

> 'I will be on the side of the people ... I will take to the barricades and the trenches, screaming as one possessed, will stain my weapons with blood, and, mad with rage, will cut the throat of any vanquished foe I encounter.'

2 What do you learn about Guevara from these quotations?

___

___

___

1.3.4 Understanding and responding to texts A and B

Guevara was a charismatic leader who was deliberate in representing himself in a particular way. He used **connotative language** powerfully to engage and inspire his audience, so that they would have a particular perspective about the type of man and leader he was.

1 From Guevara's quotations, identify a word that has a connotative meaning. (Which word conjures up emotions?)

2 In the quotations, Guevara's use of modal verbs makes his tone sound confident and assured. Find an example a modal verb that shows how likely something is to happen.

___

LANGUAGE

Connotative and denotative meanings

Words have ***connotative*** (emotional) meanings and ***denotative*** (literal) meanings. Essentially, words carry '*baggage*'. With connotations, we imply the meaning rather than stating it explicitly.

3 Find an example of a **modal verb** that is used to state when something is necessary.

4 Explain how the modal verbs reinforce Guevara's message.

LANGUAGE

Modal verbs are effective in conveying your position. Like connotations, these verbs suggest conditions on things, like ability, probability, permission and obligation. These are often known as the 'shoulda coulda woulda' verbs. They are used to change the meaning of other verbs. Knowing how people use them is essential to subtly suggest ideas. Modal verbs influence the **modality** of a text, which creates the tone of voice.

1.3.5 Expressing ideas and composing texts B

Who was Che Guevara?

1 In groups, research the life of Che Guevara. Create a timeline of up to ten major events in Guevara's life. Include two interesting ideas about him as a significant figure and one question that you would like to ask him. Use images, icons and drawings to represent some of the information on your timeline.

2 Based on your research, what is your impression of Guevara?

The *Motorcycle Diaries* is Che Guevara's diary of his journey across South America, which he did with his friend Alberto Granado in 1952. It was published after his death in 1995. The diary offers insights into Guevara's personal reflections, observations and encounters during the journey. During his travels, Guevara witnessed social injustices, poverty and inequality. The book gives us an understanding of Guevara's early life and how his experiences had a significant impact on his worldview. In 2004, the book was adapted into film.

After his death in 1967, many people saw Guevara as a hero who died for a cause. His iconic picture became a symbol of radical left-wing beliefs and opposition to imperialism.

1.3.6 Reading, viewing and listening to texts

LANGUAGE

Gaze in visual texts is used to establish a connection between the subject and viewer. There are two types of gaze: Demand and offer. ***Demand*** is where subject looks out of the image at the responder. ***Offer*** is where the figure looks away. The audience is a detached onlooker.

Study the above artwork.

1 Identify the type of **gaze** used in this image. Does Guevara look directly at the viewer?

____

____

2 What do you think this is designed to suggest about Guevara?

____

____

Writer Cory Doctorow has discussed the complexity of Guevara, explaining that we have 'Che, the man' and 'Che, the symbol' – 'Che, the man, was fierce, brilliant, flawed, vicious, and compassionate.' Che, the symbol has taken on its own personality, where many people and groups have cultivated and shaped this version over time. 'Che has become a revolutionary icon devoid of any substance, for sale on mugs and t-shirts,' says Doctorow.

Che Guevara: A Manga Biography (2010) is an illustrated graphic novel about Guevara. It was written by Kiyoshi Konno and illustrated by Chie Shimano.

CONTEXT

Chie Shimano is a manga artist in Japan and illustrator of the biography. Kiyoshi Konno is a writer and editor in Japan whose previous works have been predominately about the history of wars. Konno wrote the story of the graphic novel.

 1.3.7 Understanding and responding to texts A and B 

Since they have written a biography, Shimano and Konno have taken a stance on who they think Che Guevara is. If you get an opportunity to access this book, consider what view they have formed about him and how they represent this perspective through language and visual choices.

Let's read the blurb first …

> ‘His name is equated with rebellion, revolution, and socialism. More than forty years after his death, Che Guevara's life continues to captivate our imagination. From his childhood in Argentina and his wish to become a doctor to his encounter with Fidel Castro in 1954 and participation in the Cuban revolution, this is the extraordinary life story of a man who changed history. Told through vivid manga, this biography offers a new look at one of the world's most memorable figures.’

1 The blurb uses the inclusive pronoun ‘our’. Explain the effect this has on the reader.

____

____

2 Who is the target audience?

____

____

3 How is the reader being positioned to respond to Guevara before reading the graphic novel?

____

____

4 The contents page has five chapter headings. Look at the table and read them. Brainstorm the connotations of each of the chapter titles. What are they suggesting about Guevara?

	What are the connotations of this word?
Chapter 1: Explorer	
Chapter 2: Outsider	
Chapter 3: Guerrilla	

	What are the connotations of this word?
Chapter 4: Revolutionary	
Chapter 5: Legend	

1.3.8 Reading, viewing and listening to texts

Read the prologue.

DISCUSS

On the left-hand page, the text box comments, 'You can see him'. Discuss how the second-person address includes the reader.

IDENTIFY

Circle the images of Guevara.

DISCUSS

Discuss why Guevara's name is not on either of the first two pages of the prologue.

DISCUSS

On page two, the illustrator has used a wide panel and a close-up of the iconic Guevara portrait on the boy's t-shirt. Discuss the effect of this and how it links to the words in text box.

On these two pages, the illustrator is providing highlights of Guevara's life.

IDENTIFY

Next to each image of Guevara, write down what parts of his life it is alluding to.

DISCUSS

The images on the right are all drawn with a high angle perspective. Discuss how this positions the viewer to view Guevara.

1.3.9 Understanding and responding to texts A and B

1 The job of a prologue is to raise the reader's interest and hint at what's to come. Explain what you think the prologue is hinting at for the rest of the graphic novel.

2 Explain the perspective of Guevara that is promoted in the biography. In your response, consider the book cover, blurb, contents page and prologue. Use examples to support your ideas.

3 Do you believe the representation of Guevara is fair or biased? Explain why/why not.

How do we interpret conflicting perspectives and deal with contradictions?

The contemporary popular narrative of Che has two grossly oversimplified sides: sneering neocons who dismiss him as a butcher or a fool and denigrate those who sport Che badges as naive kids; and the worshipful reification of Che as a kind of revolutionary saint who could do no wrong.' - Cory Doctorow

So far, we have looked at one perspective of Che Guevara, which is reflective of a contemporary popular narrative. In your research, you may have come across differing perspectives. Some views dismiss Guevara as a ruthless butcher or a foolish idealist or even an unsuccessful insurgent.

1.3.10 Understanding and responding to texts A

Let's break down some of these conflicting perspectives on Che Guevara.

Heroic revolutionary	Guevara is a courageous and passionate revolutionary who is a symbol of resistance and admiration for his dedication to social change.
Cold-blooded revolutionary	Others criticise Guevara for his involvement in armed conflicts and revolutionary activities. They argue that his actions led to violence and loss of life.
Symbol of liberation	Many individuals, particularly in Latin America and other parts of the world, view Guevara as a symbol of liberation and anti-imperialism.
Authoritarian and oppressive	Some critics argue that Guevara's political ideology and approach to governance were authoritarian.
Revolutionary idealist	Some individuals perceive Guevara as an idealist who genuinely believed in creating a more egalitarian society.

Scan the QR code or research online to read 'The Killing Machine: Che Guevara' by Alvaro Vargas Llosa, and learn more about one of the contradictory perspectives of Guevara.

As you can see, perspectives on Guevara vary widely, and people may have complex and nuanced views, influenced by historical context, personal beliefs and the available information about his life and actions.

1 For each perspective, find a book, web article, song, poem or graphic novel that demonstrates the perspective.

2 Record your findings in the table. Write down the name of the text. In the 'context' column, record the who/when/where of the text. Then, provide some evidence from the text that supports this perspective.

Perspective	Text	Context	Evidence
Heroic revolutionary			
Cold-blooded revolutionary			
Symbol of liberation			

Perspective	Text	Context	Evidence
Authoritarian and oppressive			
Revolutionary idealist			

1.3.11 Expressing ideas and composing texts A and B 

So, who was the *real* Che Guevara?

1 In groups, choose a specific perspective on Guevara from the table. Collect more information that supports this perspective.

2 Conduct a class debate. *Should Guevara be seen as a hero, a 'model revolutionary who met a heroic death'? Or a brutal militarist who was 'the spokesman of a failing ideology and a ruthless executioner who did not afford others a proper legal process'?*

Consider how texts shape particular perspectives of people and how these perspectives can contradict each other. Contradictory perspectives encourage us to broaden our understanding and navigate a complex world.

Write an analytical response in which you analyse how texts shape different perspectives of Guevara. Refer to two texts to support your response. Include an introduction and one body paragraph. Remember to use a topic sentence in your body paragraph.

1.3.12 Chapter reflection

1 Which perspective(s) resonated with you the most, and why?

2 How did hearing contradicting perspectives influence your understanding of Che Guevara?

3 What challenges or complexities arise when examining historical figures with conflicting perspectives?

4 Let's return to the unit inquiry question: ***How do texts from different parts of the world reflect and shape our understanding of people, cultures and global interconnectedness?*** This chapter has encouraged you to understand that all texts present a particular view and there will often be contradictory perspectives on a topic. Contradictory perspectives can have several benefits for the global community. For example, individuals can be challenged to question their own beliefs and consider the viewpoints of others. Outline what other benefits you can think of.

Unit 1: Summative assessment

The summative assessment options below provide opportunities to demonstrate your achievement of the following outcomes and focus areas:

Outcome	EN5-RVL-01 Reading, viewing and listening to texts	EN5-URA-01 Understanding and responding to texts A	EN4-URB-01 Understanding and responding to texts B	EN5-ECA-01 Expressing ideas and composing texts A	EN5-ECB-01 Expressing ideas and composing texts B
	Reading for challenge, interest and enjoyment	Connotation, imagery and symbol	Perspective and context	Writing	Planning, monitoring and revising
				Text features	
	Reflecting			Sentence-level grammar and punctuation	
				Word-level language	

Option 1: Opinion piece

Compose an opinion piece discussing the concept of what it means to be Australian. Conduct interviews with members of your community who come from diverse backgrounds, or consider characters from film/books. Reflect on your personal experiences and observations to explore the challenges and opportunities that arise from cultural diversity. Present your findings in an opinion piece. Make sure your opinion is clear and sustained, and include relevant quotations and anecdotes to support it.

Be guided by the following questions to plan, write and produce your opinion piece.

- What is your perspective on the topic?
- What questions should you ask in your interview?
- What are the challenges and opportunities that arise from cultural diversity?
- What is the appropriate structure of an opinion piece?
- Which quotations and anecdotes can you use?
- How can you use connotation, imagery and symbols (like figurative language and devices) in your writing to help readers engage with your perspective?
- How can you craft concise sentences to enhance your writing?

Option 2: Narrative

Write a narrative in which you explore how a protagonist's experiences and backgrounds shape their perspective on the world. Include another character to provide a contrasting perspective with your protagonist. At some point in your narrative, you must include this statement: 'You must be proud you are different. Your only shame is to have shame.' Consider how your narrative can reveal the journey of your protagonist as they navigate the challenges of living in a world where they feel different.

Option 2: Narrative

Be guided by the following questions to plan, write and produce your opinion piece.

- Who is your protagonist and what is their experience and background?
- Who will be the character to provide a contrasting perspective?
- Where will you include the statement?
- Which narrative structure can you use to show your protagonist's development?
- How can you use connotation, imagery and symbols (like figurative language and devices) in your writing to help readers engage with your perspective?
- How can you craft concise sentences to enhance your writing?

Option 3: Graphic novel and reflection

Think about other historical figures or fictional characters who people have conflicting perspectives about. For example, Jack Sparrow from *The Pirates of the Caribbean*. Some people view him as a lovable rogue, while others see him as irresponsible and self-serving.

Choose one person and research as many perspectives of this person as you can. Record your findings in a mind map. Decide on the perspective that most resonates with you. Create your own two-page graphic novel prologue, representing your perspective of this figure through your visual and language choices.

Be guided by the following questions to plan, write and produce your opinion piece.

- What perspective have you presented on your historical figure or fictional character?
- What is the appropriate structure of a graphic novel?
- Which quotations, phrases and words from and about your figure can you use?
- How can you use connotation, imagery and symbols (like figurative language and devices) in your visual and language choices to help readers engage with your perspective?
- How can you craft concise sentences to enhance your writing?

These guiding questions can also be used to help you write your reflection.

Assessment as learning: self-assessment

Does my composition ...

- ☐ present a clear perspective?
- ☐ use appropriate structure?
- ☐ experiment with figurative language and devices?
- ☐ craft concise sentences?

What are two strengths of my response?

____

____

What area/s of my response do I need to refine further?

____

____

ITALY
INDIA
VISA APPROVED
LONDON
PASS FREE
EGYPT
AUSTRALIA
CANADA
ITALY
PASS FREE
LONDON
FRENCH
JAPAN
ITALY
INDIA
VISA APPROVED
LONDON
PASS FREE
EGYPT
AUSTRALIA
CANADA
PASS FREE
ITALY

UNIT
02

Issues to care about

Unit inquiry question:
How can texts promote awareness of issues and a desire to change things for the better in our world?'

In this unit, students will think critically about the ways in which quality texts can inform, persuade and challenge our understanding of current issues. It invites students to consider a range of current issues, and the role that writers can have in representing, affirming or challenging views of the world.

This unit has been broken into three chapters, each with a focus on a different current issue through both literary and non-literary extracts, including digital texts.

By exploring the central inquiry question across the three chapters, students can reflect upon a range of different issues and perspectives as well as being encouraged to consider their own position.

Chapter 4

Your world, our planet

Students will explore the issue of climate change and sustainability and how students can use their voice to raise awareness of the challenges this brings.

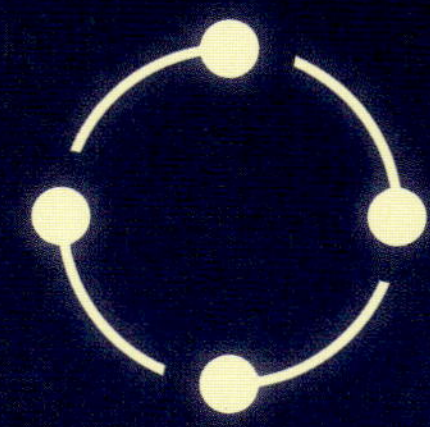

Chapter 5

Safe as houses

Students will investigate the idea of peace and security in their world by considering freedom of speech as being a right, which comes with responsibilities to use communication to help not harm.

Chapter 6

Knowledge is power

Students will examine the value of learning, education and knowledge and reflect on how these terms are similar and different. In our world, being knowledgeable can be a source of power and influence, but do we use or abuse it?

The learning activities within each chapter and the summative assessment options (on page 90) provide opportunities to assess student achievement of the following outcomes:

Outcome and Focus Area	Content point
EN5-RVL-01 Reading, viewing and listening to texts	**Reading, viewing and listening for meaning**
	Analyse the main ideas and thematic concerns represented in texts Investigate how layers of meaning are constructed in texts and how this shapes a reader's understanding and engagement Clarify and justify personal responses to texts, explaining how aspects of the text, such as character, genre, tone, salience or voice, position a reader and influence these personal responses
	Reading for challenge, interest and enjoyment
	Read increasingly complex texts that challenge thinking, pique interest, enhance enjoyment and provoke a personal response Consider how the social, cultural and ethical positions represented in texts represent, affirm or challenge views of the world Evaluate the ways reading texts help us understand ourselves and make connections to others and the world
EN5-URA-01 Understanding and responding to texts A	**Code and convention**
	Use metalanguage effectively to analyse how meaning is constructed by linguistic and stylistic elements in texts Analyse how language forms, features and structures, specific or conventional to a text's medium, context, purpose and audience, shape meaning, and experiment with this understanding through written, spoken, visual and multimodal responses
	Connotation, imagery and symbol
	Analyse how figurative language and devices can be used to represent complex ideas, thoughts and feelings to contribute to larger patterns of meaning in texts, and experiment with this in own texts
EN5-URB-01 Understanding and responding to texts B	**Perspective and context**
	Analyse how texts can be understood or interpreted from different perspectives, and experiment with this idea in own texts Explain how texts affirm or challenge established cultural attitudes and values in different contexts

EN5-ECA-01 Expressing ideas and composing texts A	**Writing**
	Select and adapt appropriate codes, conventions and structures to shape meaning when composing written texts that are analytical, informative, persuasive, discursive and/or imaginative
	Representing
	Compose visual and multimodal texts to express complex ideas, using a range of digital technologies where appropriate
	Text features
	Use the structural conventions of analytical writing purposefully, including a well-articulated and considered thesis, a sustained and cohesive progression of supporting points, and a rhetorically effective conclusion Experiment with a range of poetic forms to explore ideas and express personal perspectives
	Speaking
	Participate in and lead a range of information discussions about texts and ideas, including analytical, speculative and exploratory talk, to consolidate personal understanding and generate new ideas
EN5-ECB-01 Expressing ideas and composing texts B	**Reflecting**
	Reflect on own texts, using technical vocabulary to explain and evaluate authorial decisions appropriate to the target audience and specific purpose

CHAPTER 4

YOUR WORLD, OUR PLANET

Chapter overview

In this chapter, you will explore a range of texts, including visual texts, that delve into ideas of sustainability and protecting our planet. Poetry and speeches are a great way to express ideas that are personal and passionate, and film and artwork can convey ideas in a vibrant and immediate way.

Success criteria: In this chapter, I will be successful when I can ...

- recognise the ways in which literature can effectively communicate ideas and raise awareness of the key issues of our times
- understand the codes and conventions that characterise specific texts and the effects they can have on an audience
- reflect upon my own views on issues of the climate and how I can be more sustainable
- convey my ideas creatively and critically in my writing.

Chapter inquiry questions

- How can writers use language to raise awareness of climate change?
- How are book covers significant in communicating ideas about climate change and sustainability?
- What difference can you make?
- Can literature promote change in the relationship between humans and their natural world?

Key vocabulary

- Sustainability
- Climate change
- Climate emergency

How can writers use language to raise awareness of climate change?

Writers use language to inform, advise, persuade and entertain their audiences. Writers have the power to engage readers in discussions and debates about the important issues of our time. If you are interested in any current issues, such as climate change, try to spot how writers are engaging you to inform you about the topic, and offer a point of view.

2.4.1 Warm-up

The following words were written by Fisola Kenny-Akinnuoye, who was the runner-up in the University of Birmingham Student Climate Change Writing Competition in 2021.

Read her point of view on the role that writers can play in promoting change:

> Writers are crucial in helping us imagine a voice for what is too easily reduced to just "climate" or "environment" or "the planet". Not only do we need people who can translate the gravity of our situation but we need writers to do what they do best – to give voice to the voiceless ... to translate the language of the earth, to create empathy for our world and help construct a culture where we are connected meaningfully to this thing we call "nature".

Complete the table below and discuss with a partner.

What do you understand by her words? What images do you see?	What do you think about the point of view she offers? Do you agree or not?	What are the questions you have or solutions you wonder about when you think about protecting our planet?

How are book covers significant in communicating ideas about climate change and sustainability?

When you pick up a book to read – in a book shop or local library, or at your school – the first thing you see is the cover. Often this is what determines whether you open it and begin to read. It is important, then, that the book covers capture readers from the first moment and make them curious to read on. The Norwegian playwright Henrik Ibsen was the first to suggest that 'a picture is worth a thousand words'; never dismiss how significant a book cover can be.

2.4.2 Reading, viewing and listening to texts

Look carefully at the book covers. Go online and source the book covers for the titles Not a Drop to Drink *by Mindy McGinnis and* The New Wilderness *by Diane Cook.*

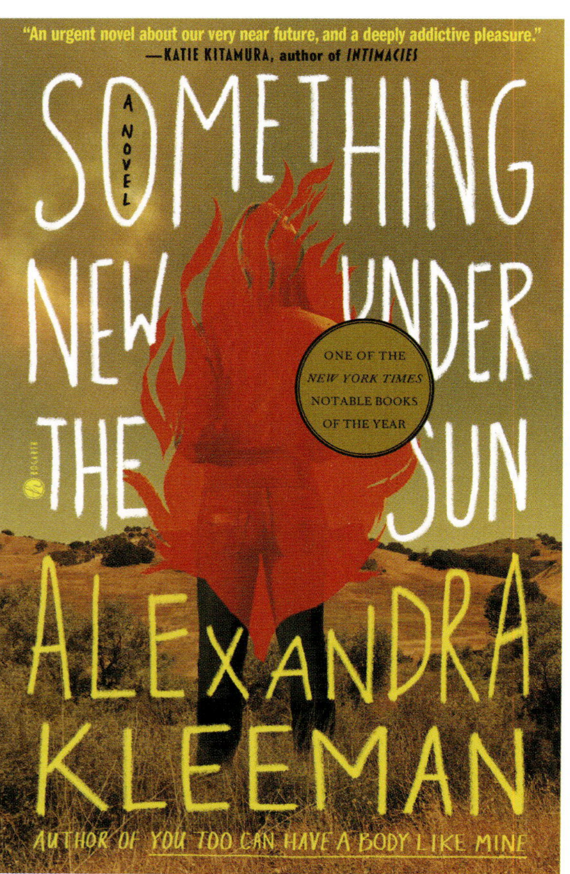

Discuss with a partner whether you think the book offers a positive or negative perspective on the ideas of climate change and sustainability.

As you talk, make sure that you justify your opinion with reference to the image.

2.4.3 Understanding and responding to texts A

After your discussion, complete the following table, which asks you to explore the codes and conventions of visual texts in the book covers.

Think about the use of composition, colour, positioning and text. Your teacher will be able to help you.

The first row has been completed as an example for you to follow:

Book cover	Environmental perspective offered	Visual technique used to illustrate this perspective	What is the effect on the audience of this technique?
Something New Under the Sun by Alexandra Kleeman	That the future will see a rise in temperatures and water will be scarce.	Contrast is shown by the juxtaposition between the orange sky, symbolising extreme heat, and the empty swimming pool, representing the scarcity of water.	This contrast serves as a warning to the viewer of the climate emergency and could make them feel angry, afraid or determined to act.
The New Wilderness by Diane Cook			
Not a Drop to Drink by Mindy McGinnis			
Please Don't Paint Our Planet Pink by Gregg Kleiner			

Extension reading

Search your school library, local bookshop or online and see if you can find any climate fiction to read. You might even be able to find these books!

Why don't you help your librarian to set up a climate fiction display or create a place online to post reviews of climate fiction that you read?

2.4.4 Reading, viewing and listening to texts

Read the following poem by American poet Amanda Gorman, aloud if you can. These words were part of her address to the United Nations General Assembly on 19 September 2022.

Scan the QR code or research online to watch Amanda Gorman's performance of this poem.

She writes this poem as an ode – this is not a happy accident!

An Ode We Owe

By Amanda Gorman

How can I ask you to do good,
When we've barely withstood
Our greatest threats yet:
The depths of death, despair and disparity,
Atrocities across cities, towns & countries,
Lives lost, climactic costs.
Exhausted, angered, we are endangered,
Not because of our numbers,
But because of our numbness. We're strangers
To one another's perils and pain,
Unaware that the welfare of the public
And the planet share a name –
– Equality
Doesn't mean being the exact same,
But enacting a vast aim:
The good of the world to its highest capability.
The wise believe that our people without power
Leaves our planet without possibility.
Therefore, though poverty is a poor existence,

VOCABULARY

Ode
noun: a lyric poem usually marked by exaltation of feeling and style, varying length of line, and complexity of stanza forms.

CONTEXT

Many people write odes as a form of inspiration. The word 'ode' originates from the Ancient Greek word for 'song'.

TECHNIQUE

In line 4 you can see a **tri-colon** or 'rule of three' used. Underline and label this technique.

TECHNIQUE

In line 6 the poet uses the technique of **assonance** which is also known as internal rhyme because it describes words that rhyme inside a line, rather than at the end.

Circle the rhyming words in this line and any other examples of assonance you notice as you read.

Complicity is a poorer excuse.
We must go the distance,
Though this battle is hard and huge,
Though this fight we did not choose,
For preserving the earth isn't a battle too large
To win, but a blessing too large to lose.
This is the most pressing truth:
That Our people have only one planet to call home
And our planet has only one people to call its own.
We can either divide and be conquered by the few,
Or we can decide to conquer the future,
And say that today a new dawn we wrote,
Say that as long as we have humanity,
We will forever have hope.
Together, we won't just be the generation
That tries but the generation that triumphs;
Let us see a legacy
Where tomorrow is not driven
By the human condition,
But by our human conviction.
And while hope alone can't save us now,
With it we can brave the now,
Because our hardest change hinges
On our darkest challenges.
Thus may our crisis be our cry, our crossroad,
The oldest ode we owe each other.
We chime it, for the climate,
For our communities.
We shall respect and protect
Every part of this planet,
Hand it to every heart on this earth,
Until no one's worth is rendered
By the race, gender, class, or identity
They were born.
This morn let it be sworn
That we are one, one human kin,
Grounded not just by the griefs
We bear, but by the good we begin.
To anyone out there:
I only ask that you care before it's too late,
That you live aware and awake,
That you lead with love in hours of hate.
I challenge you to heed this call,
I dare you to shape our fate.
Above all, I dare you to do good
So that the world might be great.

TECHNIQUE

In lines 24–25, underline the phrase that is **repeated**.

The poet **contrasts** the words 'battle' and 'blessing' – discuss with a friend why you think she does this?

INTERPRET

In lines 36–39, Gorman refers to 'the human condition'. In the context of the poem, discuss with a classmate what you think she means by these lines?

TECHNIQUE

Underline the **alliteration** in lines 42–47.

2.4.5 Understanding and responding to texts A

Look up the following nouns in your dictionary and write their meaning as an annotation on the poem.

Disparity (line 4)
Atrocities (line 5)
Complicity (line 20)
Legacy (line 36)
Kin (line 55)

1 What kinds of nouns are these?

____

____

2 Throughout the poem, Gorman uses assonance and end-stopped rhyme (end of line rhyme) – what is the effect of this on the rhythm of the poem?

____

____

____

3 In the poem, Gorman often creates the impression of the need to go to war through the language and images she uses. Highlight all the words and phrases that suggest this.

4 Choose one of these phrases and explain how it is used to persuade the audience to act on the issue of climate change.

____

____

____

____

5 What does she imagine could be the legacy of your generation (lines 36-57)?

____

____

____

____

6 What is the challenge that she uses to persuade your generation with at the end of the poem (lines 58–65)?

2.4.6 Reading, viewing and listening to texts

Gary Snyder is an American poet, environmental activist and educator. His poem 'For the Children' transports the reader to a future time, generations from now, after we have met the challenge posed to humanity by Gorman. Snyder invites us to believe in a time where children can 'go light' and are living in harmony with their environment.

Read the poem below, with a partner, aloud.

For the Children

by Gary Snyder

The rising hills, the slopes,
of statistics
lie before us.
the steep climb
of everything, going up,
up, as we all
go down.

In the next century
or the one beyond that,
they say,
are valleys, pastures,
we can meet there in peace
if we make it.

To climb these coming crests
one word to you, to
you and your children:

stay together
learn the flowers
go light

INTERPRET

Discuss with your partner how a peaceful tone is conveyed through the poet's language choices.

Underline the words and images that help to create this.

INTERPRET

At the end of this poem, Snyder gives advice to the audience – discuss this with your partner. What is it and do you think it is worth remembering?

2.4.7 Understanding and responding to texts A and B 

1 Complete the following cloze paragraph using quotational evidence from the poem. You can find suggestions in the list below:

Remember to use quotation marks when you choose from:

learn the flowers   rising hills   in peace   the next century

In the first sentence of the poem, Snyder uses a metaphor comparing the rise in statistical data we have on the worsening climate to ____________________. In stanza two, time moves forward to ____________________, where he hopes humanity will be able to meet ____________________. He gives the audience a message to unite and ____________________.

2 What perspective is Snyder giving us about climate change and the need to live sustainably?

3 In your own words, what do you think Snyder means at the end of the poem when he tells us to 'go light'?

4 Compare the two poems you have read in the chapter so far. Write a comparative paragraph showing what is similar and what is different in these poems.

You might wish to consider one of these elements to explore:

- The perspective they present of the problem and the solution.
- The language they use to convey their ideas.
- The tone of each poem, particularly at the ending.

2.4.8 Expressing ideas and composing texts A

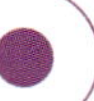

Think of an environmental issue that you know of, such as recycling, water use or renewable energy. Do some research to find out more about it.

Choose one of the activities below.

Activity 1: Write a poem expressing your perspective on this issue.

Remember that poetic language is different from prose – you should consider your line length and number, using poetic techniques such as metaphor, simile, alliteration and onomatopoeia.

You might even choose to illustrate your poem with images that complement the ideas and pictures you paint through your words like the example below:

Activity 2: Design a book cover for one of the poems you have read in this chapter.

Consider the key message of the poem and how you could communicate it in visual form. You could focus on a particular image that resonated with you as you were reading and discussing.

Think about the visual devices that will be most effective – composition, colour, positioning, font and image choices.

What difference can you make?

Our twenty-first century is all about empowerment and having a voice for change. We live in a digital world, and our global connection is a powerful tool to influence hearts and minds. Harness your world to make the change you seek!

2.4.9 Expressing ideas and composing texts B

'What difference can I make?'

'It's not my problem!'

'Why should I have to sort out the mess of generations before me?'

Sound familiar? Let's start thinking about what you can do to make a difference in the climate change debate.

1 What is a 'carbon footprint'?

____

____

2 With a partner, discuss the different actions that can increase or decrease a carbon footprint. On one footprint, write the actions that increase it and on the other the actions that decrease it.

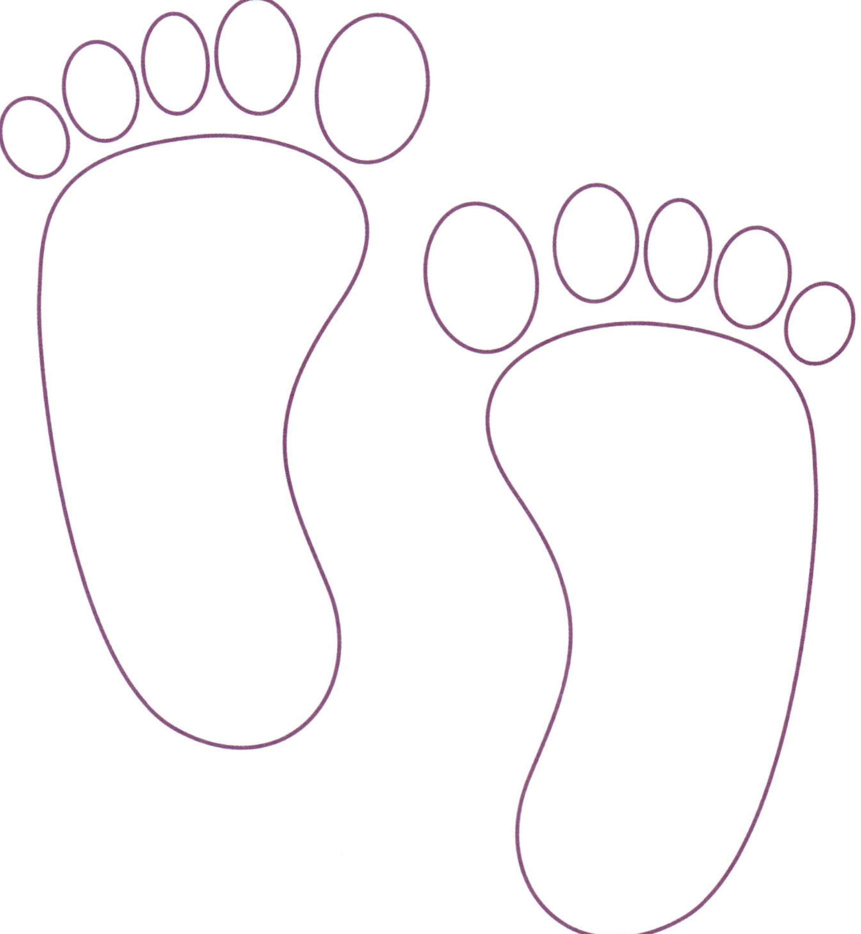

CIRCLES OF POSSIBILITY ACTIVITY

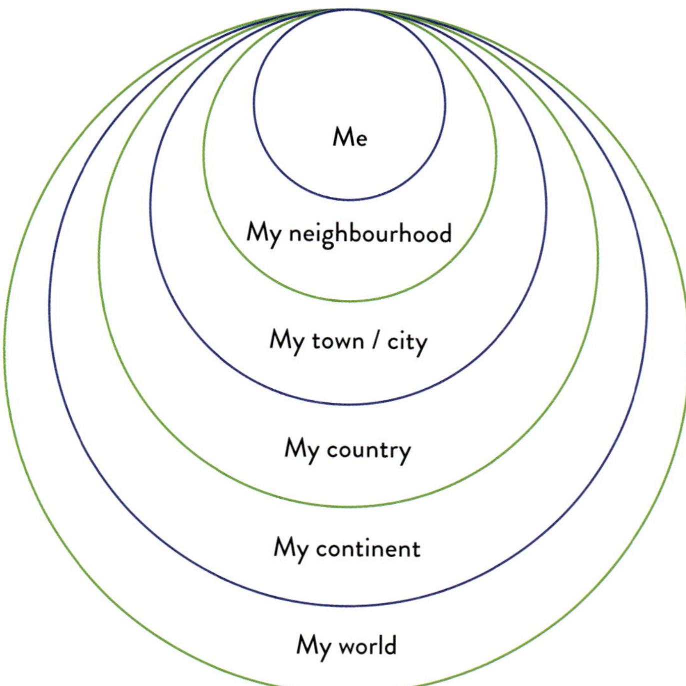

In a small group, discuss one effect of climate change that you know about.

Fill in the 'circles of possibility' diagram, starting with how this effect affects you. Fill out each circle until you reach the outside 'My world' circle.

Indian social activist Mahatma Gandhi said, 'If we could change ourselves, the tendencies in the world would also change. As a man changes his own nature, so does the attitude of the world change towards him.'

If you could change or begin to do three things that would have a positive impact on the environment what would they be?

1 ____

2 ____

3 ____

Extension activity

Stage 1

Work with others in your class to identify an area of your school that could be more sustainable. This might be starting up a vegetable garden, setting up recycling bins around the school and ensuring they are collected by the council, or asking your school canteen to only use recyclable packaging.

Stage 2

Brainstorm ways in which you could raise awareness in your school community about your issue. This might be posters, surveys or a letter to your principal.

Stage 3

Choose at least one of these ideas, put it into practice and see if you can be a force for change in your school!

GOOD LUCK!

Can literature promote change in the relationship between humans and their natural world?

In this chapter you have been offered several different writers' perspectives about climate change and how you have been charged with protecting our planet. These writers believe we are all guardians of our home, that with the privilege of being here also comes a collective responsibility to promote change to protect and preserve it.

What do you think?

2.4.10 Chapter reflection

Our perspectives and experiences of the effects of climate change and the benefits of sustainability are varied, but many writers and artists believe that we all have a part to play in protecting our planet from future harm.

How have the writers you have read in this unit tried to communicate this message to you?

Composer	The composers aimed to challenge their audiences to think deeply about issues of climate and sustainability. On a scale of 1–5 how successful do you think they were? Justify your rating with reference to the extract.
Fisola Kenny-Akinnuoye	
Amanda Gorman	

Gary Snyder	
Book cover artists (you can focus on one or comment on them all)	

Let's return to the unit inquiry question: ***How can texts promote awareness of issues and a desire to change things for the better in our world?*** How have these four texts broadened or challenged your understanding of climate issues and sustainability?

CHAPTER 5

SAFE AS HOUSES

Chapter overview

This chapter considers ideas about peace and conflict and how we can and do use, and have used, our powers of communication to raise awareness, promote our beliefs and values and inspire others.

You will be asked to think about how rhetorical techniques can be used to influence those around us and how our language choices, in a variety of different contexts, can both help and harm.

Success criteria: In this chapter, I will be successful when I can ...

- recognise how writers use language to promote different values towards others
- understand that rhetorical language can be used to promote a particular perspective in a text
- reflect on how the language used in digital interactions can be both positive and negative.

Chapter inquiry questions

- Is our world a battlefield?
- How do our words communicate our values?
- How can using rhetoric promote your beliefs?
- How do we harness social media as a tool for peace?

Key vocabulary

- Empathy
- Rhetoric
- Freedom of expression

2.5.1 Warm-up with a partner!

Read the **idioms** in the table below and try to work out their meaning together if you haven't heard of them before.

Rewrite them in Standard Australian English in the column provided.

LANGUAGE

Idiom

This chapter is called 'Safe as houses' because it explores ideas about war and peace in our world. The phrase 'safe as houses' is an ***idiom***, which is a phrase containing a figurative meaning that often differs from its literal one. This particular idiom dates from Victorian times when the idea that investment in property was seen to be the safest way to secure your fortune.

Idiom	Meaning
Cut someone some slack	
To get bent out of shape	
Birds of a feather flock together	
Let the cat out of the bag	
The elephant in the room	

Is our world a battlefield?

As we look around, every time we turn on our TVs or go online, we are aware of conflicts around the world. Sometimes it seems as though there are wars happening all the time and it can be hard to understand why people are fighting so far away and why we should care.

2.5.2 Reading, viewing and listening to texts

Scan the QR code or go online and explore the Global Conflict Tracker website.

Discuss and brainstorm your response to the inquiry question: 'Is our world a battlefield?' Write notes in the box below.

You can discuss:

Is our world a battlefield?

1 Where are the different conflicts in the world and what they are about?

2 How long have these conflicts been going on?

3 What has been the impact on everyday people in the conflict zone and/or beyond it?

2.5.3 Understanding and responding to texts A and B

Conflicts in our world are not a recent thing at all. The twentieth century saw two World Wars and Australia was involved in wars in Vietnam and Korea. More recently we have been hearing a lot about the war in Ukraine. Writers and artists have been at the forefront of both supporting and disagreeing with these conflicts – using their right of freedom of expression to do so.

Writers and poets on the 'home front' often used their words to promote patriotism and encourage young men to join up as soldiers. They used words and images of glory and victory to persuade and inspire.

However, anti-war poetry has long been used as a vehicle to challenge the status quo and to evoke empathy through vivid imagery and emotive language. This can lead to increased awareness of the horrors of war and public opposition to conflict, thus influencing political and social movements.

The poet Siegfried Sassoon wrote about World War 1 (1914–1918) from the perspective of the soldiers. He offers a point of view of the reality of war for the men who were on the front line.

Read his poem 'Attack', then respond to the questions below.

Attack

By Siegfried Sassoon

At dawn the ridge emerges massed and **dun**
In the wild purpose of the glow'ring sun,
Smouldering through spouts of drifting smoke that shroud
The menacing scarred slope; and, one by one,
Tanks creep and topple forward to the wire.
The **barrage** roars and lifts. Then, clumsily bowed
With bombs and guns and shovels and battle-gear,
Men **jostle** and climb to, meet the bristling fire.
Lines of grey, muttering faces, masked with fear,
They leave their **trenches**, going over the top,
While time ticks blank and busy on their wrists,
And hope, with **furtive** eyes and grappling fists,
Flounders in mud. O Jesus, make it stop!

VOCABULARY

Dun
adjective: a greyish-brown colour.

Barrage
noun: a focused military bombardment over a wide area. In World War 1 and 2 barrage balloons were also released into the air to cause a hazard for low flying bombing aircraft.

Jostle
verb: push and shove forwards in a disorganised way.

Trenches
noun: in World War 1 soldiers lived in an intricate labyrinth of trenches dug into the earth, only coming out of them to fight and try to gain more ground in battle.

Furtive
adjective: an action done in a quiet and secretive way to avoid being noticed.

Flounders
verb: slips and slides, unable to gain a firm footing.

1 In the following lines, circle the repeated letter or sound. (This repeated sound/letter is an example of the technique of **sibilance**.)

> 'Smouldering through spouts of drifting smoke that shroud
> The menacing scarred slope;'

2 What effect do you think Sassoon is trying to create by using **sibilance**?

___

___

___

___

3 The words 'menacing' and 'creep' in lines 4 and 5 create a feeling of danger for the soldiers in this poem. Explain how these words use **personification** to try to do that.

4 In the second half of the poem, what words and phrases are used by Sassoon to create **empathy** with the soldiers? Write them in the space below:

5 In this poem, Sassoon is promoting awareness about the plight of soldiers in battle. Explain what **perspective** about war is being offered by Sassoon by presenting the soldiers in this way? Try to refer to the ideas and language in the poem to justify your ideas.

How do our words communicate our values?

After World War 2 (1939–1945) there was great public enthusiasm for peace, and the United Nations was born. The United Nations was a voice to advocate for international cooperation and to maintain international peace and security. Their Charter was signed on 26 June 1945 and today has 193 member states who are all bound to its core purpose.

 2.5.4 Understanding and responding to texts A and B

Read the opening of the Charter below.

WE THE PEOPLES OF THE UNITED NATIONS DETERMINED

to save succeeding generations from the scourge of war, which twice in our lifetime has brought untold sorrow to mankind, and

to reaffirm faith in fundamental human rights, in the dignity and worth of the human person, in the equal rights of men and women and of nations large and small, and

to establish conditions under which justice and respect for the obligations arising from treaties and other sources of international law can be maintained, and

to promote social progress and better standards of life in larger freedom,

AND FOR THESE ENDS

to practice tolerance and live together in peace with one another as good neighbours, and

to unite our strength to maintain international peace and security, and

to ensure, by the acceptance of principles and the institution of methods, that armed force shall not be used, save in the common interest, and

to employ international machinery for the promotion of the economic and social advancement of all peoples,

HAVE RESOLVED TO COMBINE OUR EFFORTS TO ACCOMPLISH THESE AIMS.

Accordingly, our respective Governments, through representatives assembled in the city of San Francisco, who have exhibited their full powers found to be in good and due form, have agreed to the present Charter of the United Nations and do hereby establish an international organization to be known as the United Nations.

Let's have a look at this extract to see the language used to reflect the values of war and peace.

1 In the first section, identify two phrases used to describe war.

____

____

2 In the first section, identify two words or phrases that embody the values of the United Nations.

____

____

3 In the second section, underline the phrases that show what ideals the UN promotes as ways to avoid future wars?

____

____

4 **What do you notice about the perspective towards war and peace offered here through the language choices made? Justify your response with reference to the extract.**

In the final paragraph, the Charter recognises that each representative country will have a voice to express fears or concerns of war and to be a voice for peace.

The ideal of freedom of expression dates back to the time of ancient Greece and our world's first democracies. It comes from the Ancient Greek word, 'parrhesia' which means 'to speak candidly'. Freedom of speech is enshrined in the American Constitution, and the Australian High Court upholds free speech as integral to our society.

Freedom of speech allows us to communicate what we believe to the world on a variety of platforms – in print, in film and in speeches to inspire and persuade others to our point of view.

How can using rhetoric promote your beliefs?

Rhetoric is a style of verbal and written communication that uses different features to inform, persuade or inspire an audience. Politicians, motivational speakers and even you use rhetoric when you want to promote a particular belief, value or point of view.

Some key rhetorical devices are:

Repetition involves the intentional use of words, phrases or ideas multiple times for emphasis or to reinforce your perspective. It can create a sense of rhythm, build anticipation or emphasise key ideas.

Hyperbole is an exaggerated statement or claim that is not meant to be taken literally. It is used to create emphasis or make a point more strongly.

Pathos is using language that appeals to an audience's emotions and can include using vivid imagery to shock or emotive language to evoke pity.

Logos includes the use of statistical data to make your perspective have greater credibility with an audience.

2.5.5 Reading, viewing and listening to texts

Scan the QR code to watch Malala Yousafzai's 16th birthday speech to the United Nations.

Read the extract below from Malala Yousafzai's 16th birthday speech to the United Nations. She uses her newly-found freedom of expression to promote her values and beliefs of peace over war. Access and view this speech online, then respond to the activity questions.

There are hundreds of human rights activists and social workers who are not only speaking for human rights, but who are struggling to achieve their goals of education, peace and equality. Thousands of people have been killed by the terrorists and millions have been injured. I am just one of them.

So here I stand, one girl among many.

I speak not for myself, but for all girls and boys.

I raise up my voice – not so that I can shout, but so that those without a voice can be heard.

Those who have fought for their rights:

Their right to live in peace. Their right to be treated with dignity. Their right to equality of opportunity. Their right to be educated.

Dear Friends, on the 9th of October 2012, the Taliban shot me on the left side of my forehead. They shot my friends too. They thought that the bullets would silence us. But they failed. And then, out of that silence came, thousands of voices. The terrorists thought that they would change our aims and stop our ambitions but nothing changed in my life except this: Weakness, fear and hopelessness died. Strength, power and courage was born. I am the same Malala. My ambitions are the same. My hopes are the same. My dreams are the same.

Dear sisters and brothers, I am not against anyone. Neither am I here to speak in terms of personal revenge against the Taliban or any other terrorists group. I am here to speak up for the right of education of every child. I want education for the sons and the daughters of all the extremists especially the Taliban.

I do not even hate the Talib who shot me. Even if there is a gun in my hand and he stands in front of me. I would not shoot him. This is the compassion that I have learnt from Muhammad – the prophet of mercy, Jesus Christ and Lord Buddha. This is the legacy of change that I have inherited from Martin Luther King, Nelson Mandela and Muhammad Ali Jinnah. This is the philosophy of non-violence that I have learnt from Gandhi Jee, Bacha Khan and Mother Teresa. And this is the forgiveness that I have learnt from my mother and father. This is what my soul is telling me, be peaceful and love everyone.

Dear sisters and brothers, we realise the importance of light when we see darkness. We realise the importance of our voice when we are silenced. In the same way, when we were in Swat, the north of Pakistan, we realised the importance of pens and books when we saw the guns.

2.5.6 Understanding and responding to texts A and B 

1 At the start of her speech, Malala says:

> 'I speak not for myself, but for all girls and boys.
>
> I raise up my voice – not so that I can shout, but so that those without a voice can be heard.'

She is using 'my voice' as a noun here and as a metaphor. For what?

2 She goes on to say:

> 'Their right to live in peace. Their right to be treated with dignity. Their right to equality of opportunity. Their right to be educated.'

a Highlight the repetition in this quotation. What do you notice about it?

b This rhetorical technique is a kind of repetition known as **symploce**. What effect does it have on the audience?

3 Consider her words:

> 'My ambitions are the same. My hopes are the same. My dreams are the same.'

a Highlight the repetition in his quotation. What do you notice about it?

b This rhetorical device is another kind of repetition known as **epistrophe** or **epiphora**. What effect does it have on the way the audience views Malala?

4 Read the highlighted paragraph again. In this paragraph, Malala alludes to religious figures and leaders of civil rights. Write the names of the ones you can spot below.

a By including these **allusions**, what do you think Malala is trying to communicate to her audience about her values and beliefs?

5 In the final paragraph, Malala says: 'we realise the importance of light when we see darkness.'

a What literary device do you recognise here?

b How does this communicate ideas about freedom of expression and ideas of peace?

2.5.7 Expressing ideas and composing texts A

Overall, how successfully do you think Malala uses a variety of rhetorical techniques to communicate her values about war and peace, and to promote a change in people's attitudes? Justify your response with close reference to the speech extract.

You could structure your ideas using the following scaffold for analytical writing.

PETAL TECHNIQUE

- **P** Build the **p**oint/s you are analysing and why
- **E** Provide **e**vidence to support your argument
- **T** Identify the **t**echnique
- **A** **A**nalyse your point and prove your argument
- **L** Conclude and **l**ink back to your point

How do we harness social media as a tool for peace?

In this chapter you have thought about how words can be used to raise awareness about the conditions of war and to advocate for peace through expressing ourselves freely.

We have seen how people can raise up their voice through poetry, charters and speeches to communicate their values and beliefs about the need to create a world of harmony.

Social media is an easy and immediate way to express opinions and communicate with others in our digital world.

2.5.8 Reading, viewing and listening to texts

Get into groups of three. Each group member should go online and visit the websites for the following organisations: Mercy Corps, Seeds for Peace and Kids for Peace.

After you have explored these organisations, discuss with your group members the ways in which you have seen digital texts being used to promote peace and create a safer world for everyone.

2.5.9 Chapter reflection

This chapter has asked you to consider how we can use language to influence others. Reflect on some of the ways that the texts you have encountered have done this, and write a short paragraph explaining which you think has been the most effective at conveying ideas of peace/war and why.

Issues to care about

Remember your texts were:

- the Global Conflict Tracker website
- a poem by Siegfried Sassoon
- an extract from the United Nations Charter
- a speech from Malala Yousafzai.

As a starting point, you might like to consider:

- the message delivered and its relevance to you and your world
- the mode of delivery
- the composer's use of rhetorical devices.

Let's return to the unit inquiry question: ***How can texts promote awareness and change about issues in our world?*** How have these four texts broadened or challenged your understanding of peace and war?

Chapter 6

Knowledge is Power

Chapter overview

This chapter explores the value of learning, education and knowledge and asks you to reflect on how these terms are similar and different. Through texts, you will investigate barriers to education and knowledge, how these can be overcome and the impact of education on individuals and societal well-being. You will be asked to reflect on your own learning journey and how your education has shaped you.

Success criteria: In this chapter, I will be successful when I can ...

- distinguish between learning and education
- recognise the challenges some people have accessing learning
- interpret a character's thoughts and feelings and how this reflects their values
- develop a character's 'voice' in a first-person narrative
- reflect on the purpose of education in a modern world.

Chapter inquiry questions

- Are education, learning and knowledge the same?
- Why educate?
- What are the barriers to education?
- Can barriers to education be overcome?

Key vocabulary

- Education
- Learning
- Narrative voice
- Interpretation

Are education, learning and knowledge the same?

Think about your life journey so far.

As soon as you are born you begin to learn – to smile, to walk, to talk. Learning is a gradual process that happens throughout our lives. We are constantly learning; it is instinctive, although we might not always realise it is happening.

Through learning you gain knowledge – knowledge about yourself and the people and places in your world, and skills that will help you survive and thrive. Knowledge comes from your experiences, from your 'real-life' interactions and challenges. It can seem that knowledge is an end-point in our learning, but by reflecting on knowledge we can continue to learn.

Education is one context in which we can learn and acquire knowledge. In life there are no rules, restrictions or boundaries to learning and gaining knowledge, but in education knowledge is usually given to us by others within clear structures set by a specific curriculum at a school or university. Education can be helpful to compartmentalise learning.

3.6.1 Warm-up

Think about your life journey so far.

In the Venn diagram below, brainstorm what you have learned so far, what knowledge you have gained through life-learning and through educational-learning. In the overlap, jot down what knowledge has been learned by both.

You can see an example to get you started:

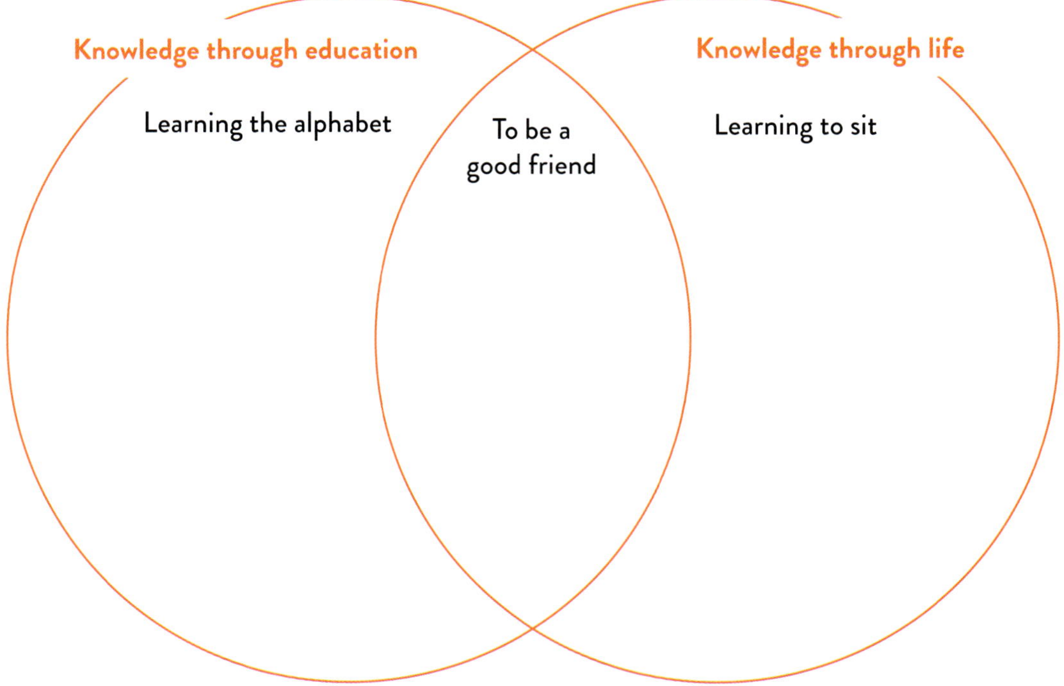

Why educate?

In Unit 2, Chapter 5 you read a speech in which Malala Yousafzai stated that she wanted 'the right of education of every child' because she believes that through education we can the solve the problems we face in the world.

In the US, education was made compulsory in 1852 ... but only up until the age of 14 and only for 3 months a year!

In the UK, education became compulsory in 1880 ... but only to age of 10!

Australia is ahead of both – education became compulsory in 1872, and students had to stay in school until the age of 15 unless they had a reasonable excuse.

DISCUSS

Discuss with a partner:

Teenagers, parents, teachers and employers often have different views on why education is important, or not.

Read the quotations below and discuss each one with a partner or in a small group – a good starting point is deciding how far you agree or disagree with each statement.

Make sure that you record your ideas in a separate notebook.

Why is education important?

'The more that you read, the more things you will know, the more that you learn, the more places you'll go.' – Dr. Seuss

'Education breeds confidence. Confidence breeds hope. Hope breeds peace.' – Confucius

'Give a man a fish and you feed him for a day; teach a man to fish and you feed him for a lifetime.' – Maimonides

'The aim of education is the knowledge, not of facts, but of values.' – William S. Burroughs

3.6.2 Expressing ideas and composing texts A

Write a reflective response that articulates your thinking and discussions so far. Demonstrate your understanding of the words 'education', 'learning' and 'knowledge', and how they are similar and different. You may need to complete this in a separate notebook if you run out of room here.

____

____

____

____

____

____

____

____

What are the barriers to education?

Whenever we read a text we can infer the meaning through the writer's language choices. From these inferences we build an interpretation of characters and events.

As you read the short story below, you will be asked to consider how the writer is encouraging you to build an interpretation that will help you understand the ideas of education more deeply.

The Scholarship Jacket

By Martha Salinas

The small Texas school that I attended carried out a tradition every year during the eighth grade graduation: a beautiful gold and green jacket, the school colors, was awarded to the class valedictorian, the student who had maintained the highest grade for eight years. The scholarship jacket had a big gold S on the left front side and the winner's name was written in gold letters on the pocket.

INTERPRET

Why do you think the character is so desperate to win this jacket?

My oldest sister Rosie had won the jacket a few years back and I fully expected to win also. I was fourteen and in the eighth grade. I had been a straight A student since the first grade, and the last year I had looked forward to owning that jacket. My father was a farm laborer who couldn't earn enough money to feed eight children, so when I was six I was given to my grandparents to raise. We couldn't participate in sports in school because there were registration fees, uniform costs, and trips out of town; so even though we were quite agile and athletic there would never be a sports school jacket for us. This one, the scholarship jacket, was our only chance.

Circle the inclusive pronoun in this sentence.

In May, close to graduation, spring fever struck, and no one paid any attention in class; instead we stared out the windows and at each other, wanting to speed up the last few weeks of school. I despaired every time I looked in the mirror. Pencil thin, not a curve anywhere, I was called 'Beanpole' and 'String Bean' and I knew that's what I looked like. A flat chest, no hips, and a brain, that's what I had. That really isn't much for a fourteen-year-old to work with, I thought, as I absentmindedly wandered from my history class in the gym. Another hour of sweating in basketball and displaying my toothpick legs was coming up. Then I remembered my P.E. shorts were still in a bag under my desk where I'd forgotten them. I had to walk all the way back and get them. Coach Thompson was a real bear if anyone wasn't dressed for P.E. She had said I was a good forward and once she even tried to talk Grandma into letting me join the team. Grandma, of course, said no.

NARRATIVE VOICE

Think about how the first-person narrative helps the reader gain greater knowledge about the story's central character.

TECHNIQUE

What is the technique used here?

I was almost back at my classroom's door when I heard angry voices and arguing. I stopped. I didn't mean to eavesdrop; I just hesitated, not knowing what to do. I needed those shorts and I was going to be late, but I didn't want to interrupt an argument between my teachers. I recognized the voices; Mr. Schmidt, my history teacher, and Mr. Boone, my maths teacher. They seemed to be arguing about me. I couldn't believe it. I still remember the shock that rooted me flat against the wall as if I were trying to blend in with the graffiti written there.

'I refuse to do it! I don't care who her father is, her grades don't even begin to compare to Martha's. I won't lie or falsify records. Martha has a straight A plus average and you know it!' That was Mr. Schmidt and he sounded very angry. Mr. Boone's voice sounded calm and quiet.

'Look, Joann's father is not only on the Board, he owns the only store in town; we could say it was a close tie and ...'

The pounding in my ears drowned out the rest of the words; only a word here and there filtered through. '... Martha is Mexican ... resign ... won't do it ...' Mr. Schmidt came rushing out, luckily for me went down the opposite way toward the auditorium, so he didn't see me.

INTERPRET

What do you think this conversation is about?

Shaking, I waited a few minutes and then went in and grabbed my bag and fled from the room. Mr. Boone looked up when I came in but didn't say anything. To this day I don't remember if l got in trouble in P.E. for being late or how I made it through the rest of the afternoon. I went home very sad and cried into my pillow that night so grandmother wouldn't hear me. It seemed a cruel coincidence that I had overheard that conversation.

The next day when the principal called me into the office, I knew what it would be about. He looked uncomfortable and unhappy. I decided I wasn't going to make it easier for him so I looked him straight in the eye. He looked away and fidgeted with the papers on his desk.

'Martha,' he said, 'there's been a change in policy this year regarding the scholarship jacket. As you know, it has always been free.' He cleared his throat and continued. 'This year the Board decided to charge fifteen dollars – which still won't cover the complete cost of the jacket.'

I stared at him in shock and a small sound of dismay escaped my throat. I hadn't expected this. He still avoided looking in my eyes.

'So if you are unable to pay the fifteen dollars for the jacket, it will be given to the next one in line.'

Standing with all the dignity I could muster, I said, 'I'll speak to my grandfather about it, sir, and let you know tomorrow.'

INTERPRET

What has the character learned about education by the Principal's action?

I cried on the walk home from the bus stop. The dirt road was a quarter of a mile from the highway, so by the time I got home, my eyes were red and puffy.

'Where's Grandpa?' I asked Grandma, looking down at the floor so she wouldn't ask me why I'd been crying. She was sewing on a quilt and didn't look up.

'I think he's out back working in the bean field.'

I went outside and looked out at the fields. There he was, I could see him walking between the rows, his body bent over the little plants, hoe in hand. I walked slowly out to him, trying to think of how I could best ask him for the money. There was a cool breeze blowing and a sweet smell of mesquite in the air, but I didn't appreciate it. I kicked at a dirt clot. I wanted that jacket so much. It was more than just being a valedictorian and giving a little thank you speech for the jacket on graduation night. It represents eight years of hard work and expectation. I knew I had to be honest with Grandpa; it was my only chance. He saw me and looked up.

He waited for me to speak. I cleared my throat nervously and clasped my hands behind my back so he wouldn't see them shaking. 'Grandpa, I have a big favor to ask you,' I said in Spanish, the only language he knew. He still waited silently, I tried again. 'Grandpa, this year the principal said the scholarship jacket is not going to be free. It's going to cost fifteen dollars and I have to take the money tomorrow, otherwise it'll be given to someone else.' The last words came out in an eager rush. Grandpa straightened up tiredly and leaned his chin on the hoe handle. He looked out over the field that was filled with the tiny green bean plants. I waited, desperately hoping he'd say I could have the money. He turned to me and asked quietly, 'What does a scholarship jacket mean?'

I answered quickly; maybe there was a chance. 'It means you've earned it by having the highest grades for eight years and that's why they're giving it to you.' Too late I realized the significance of my words. Grandpa knew that I understood it was not a matter of money. It wasn't that. He went back to hoeing the weeds that sprang up between the dedicated little bean plants. It was a time consuming job; sometimes the small shoots were right next to each other. Finally he spoke again.

'Then if you pay for it, Marta, it's not a scholarship jacket, is it? Tell your principal I will not pay the fifteen dollars.'

INTERPRET

Why does Martha's grandfather refuse to pay for the jacket?

I walked back to the house and locked myself in the bathroom for a long time. I was angry with grandfather even though I know he was right; and I was angry with the Board, whoever they were. Why did they have to change the rules just when it was my turn to win the jacket?

It was a very sad and withdrawn girl who dragged into the principal's office the next day. This time he did look me in the eyes.

'What did your grandfather say?' I sat very straight in my chair. 'He said to tell you he won't pay the fifteen dollars.'

The principal muttered something I couldn't understand under his breath, and walked over to the window. He stood looking out at something outside. He looked bigger than usual when he stood up; he was a tall gaunt man with gray hair, and I watched the back of his head while I waited for him to speak.

'Why?' he finally asked. 'Your grandfather has the money. Doesn't he own a small bean farm?'

I looked at him, forcing my eyes to stay dry. 'He said if I had to pay for it, then it wouldn't be a scholarship jacket,' I said and stood up to leave. 'I guess you'll just have to give it to Joann.' I hadn't meant to say that; it had just slipped out. I was almost to the door when he stopped me.

'Martha – wait.'

I turned and looked at him, waiting. What did he want now? I could feel my heart pounding. Something bitter and vile tasting was corning up in my mouth; I was afraid I was going to be sick. I didn't need any sympathy speeches. He sighed loudly at me, biting his lip, as if thinking.

'Okay, damn it. We'll make an exception in your case. I'll tell the Board, you'll get your jacket.'

I could hardly believe it. I spoke in a trembling rush. 'Oh, thank you sir!' Suddenly I felt great. I didn't know about adrenalin in those days, but I knew something was pumping through me, making me feel as tall as the sky. I wanted to yell, jump, run the mile, do something. I ran out so I could cry in the hall where there was no one to see me. At the end of the day, Mr. Schmidt winked at me and said, 'I hear you're getting a scholarship jacket this year.' His face looked as happy and innocent as a baby's but I knew better. Without answering I gave him a quick hug and ran to the bus. I cried on the walk home again, but this time because I was so happy. I couldn't wait to tell Grandpa and ran straight to the field. I joined him in row where he was working and without saying anything I crouched down and started pulling up the weeds with my hands. Grandpa worked alongside me for a few minutes, but he didn't ask what had happened. After I had a little pile of weeds between the rows, I stood up and faced him.

'The principal said he's making an exception for me, Grandpa, and I'm getting the jacket after all. That's after I told him what you said.'

Grandpa didn't say anything; he just gave me a pat on the shoulder and a smile. He pulled out the crumpled red handkerchief that he always carried in his back pocket and wiped the sweat off his forehead.

'Better go see if your grandmother needs any help with supper.'

I gave him a big grin. He didn't fool me. I skipped and ran back to the house whistling some silly tune.

INTERPRET

How does the first-person voice limit the reader's understanding of what the principal is thinking?

INTERPRET

Why do you think the principal changed his mind?

INTERPRET

Why is Martha so happy?

INTERPRET

What does Martha mean by the words, 'He didn't fool me?'

3.6.3 Understanding and responding to texts B

1 What were the different barriers that the main character experienced in this short story? Who presented them, and how did she overcome them?

You should use quotations from the story to justify your thinking and organise your ideas logically to respond to the questions of what, who and how.

2 What do you think she learned about

a herself

b others through this experience?

Can barriers to education be overcome?

In 'The Scholarship Jacket' Martha experienced a range of challenges posed by others. Sometimes the challenges preventing us from learning can be small or huge. They are often overcome by our own commitment and persistence to learn.

3.6.4 Reading, viewing and listening to texts

Research the story of Kimani Maruge who was 84 when he first attended school in Kenya. Although access to education in many African countries has improved, the continent's literacy rate overall is the lowest in the world. So it will be a good idea to find out about this broader context as well as Maruge's life.

As you read about his story, write down six surprising or interesting pieces of knowledge that you learn.

Watch the trailer for The First Grader, *a movie about Maruge's experience, by scanning the QR code below or researching online.*

After viewing this trailer, discuss how the story of Maruge embodies the ideas of knowledge, learning and education.

As you discuss, you might want to consider:

- how the children reacted to the news of universal education in Kenya
- the barriers Maruge experienced trying to access knowledge through education
- how Maruge's persistence and commitment revealed his values towards learning.

3.6.5 Expressing ideas and composing texts A

When you read 'The Scholarship Jacket' you thought about some of the advantages and disadvantages of writing a first-person narrative. One of the good things about the first-person is that the reader can experience the character's thoughts and feelings as they do, and this can make an unfamiliar experience easier for the reader to understand.

Imagine you are either Kimani Maruge or a pupil in the school he attended.

Write a diary entry as your chosen character that intentionally reveals their attitude towards learning and education by describing a typical day at school.

You should write in the first-person narrative voice and use the past tense.

3.6.6 Chapter reflection

In Australia, many young people are learning full-time until the age of 17. This means that, at a minimum, you are likely to be at school for twelve years. Inevitably, your school, your teachers and the learning experiences you have had will have had an impact on what you know and see as valuable, your future goals and how you will lead your life as an adult.

1 **Create an artwork, poem or short story that reveals how your own education has influenced your values and aspirations.**

Now reflect on your writing:

2 Note two authorial choices you made in your artwork/poem/short story and comment on how they reflect the influence of your learning and education.

Let's return to the unit inquiry question: ***How can texts promote awareness and change about issues in our world?*** How have your reading experiences in this chapter addressed the inquiry question?

Unit 2: Summative assessment

The summative assessment options below provide opportunities to demonstrate your achievement of the following outcomes and focus areas:

Outcome	EN5-RVL-01 Reading, viewing and listening to texts	EN5-URA-01 Understanding and responding to texts A	EN4-URB-01 Understanding and responding to texts B	EN5-ECA-01 Expressing ideas and composing texts A	EN5-ECB-01 Expressing ideas and composing texts B
	Reading, viewing and listening for meaning	Code and convention	Perspective and context	Writing	Reflecting
				Representing	
	Reading for challenge, interest and enjoyment	Connotation, imagery and symbol		Text features	
				Speaking	

Option 1: Imaginative writing

Read the poem below and use its ideas to inspire a piece of original writing – a short story or poem – that explores the world of the last human. You could write a first-person narrative as the last human being or assume the voice of Nature.

When the Last Human Being

By Francis Duggan

When the last human being from Planet Earth has gone
The Goddess of Nature will surely live on
Yes without us to bother her Nature will live
We take and take from her and in return little give
For our disrespect to her we will be made to pay
What goes around comes around as some do say
Nature for her extinct life forms never lament
The dinosaurs came and the dinosaurs went
She gives life and the remains of her dead does receive
And in the face of death she does not laugh or grieve
But long after the last human being from the World has gone
Nature the immortal will be living on.

Be guided by the following questions to plan, write and produce your imaginative writing.

- Who is the voice leading your writing?
- What do they have to say about the relationship between humans and the natural world?
- How are you organising your paragraphs or stanzas to ensure a logical sequence?
- Have you used vocabulary that enhances the style of writing you have chosen and shapes meaning for the reader?
- Have you considered how varying your sentence types, sentence lengths and punctuation can enhance your reader's experience?

Option 2: Online feature article

Throughout the world, many people struggle and fight to access education due to a range of reasons such as geographical location, gender inequality, prejudice and poverty.

In Australia, there are students in rural communities who also struggle to access education, particularly in Aboriginal and Torres Strait Islander communities. Many organisations such as Save the Children and World Vision facilitate programmes around Australia to alleviate barriers to education. There are also local programmes, such as Ngaliya on the NSW Central Coast, with the same aim.

Research one of these organisations or one in your local area and write an online feature article.

Be guided by the following questions to plan, write and produce your feature article.

- How does your article inform the public about the barriers to education?
- Have you used rhetorical devices to persuade your audience that your organisation can make a real difference in the lives of young Australians?
- Do your authorial choices inspire your audience to help or get involved in your chosen program?

Have you used a style suitable to the text type? Remember that online texts have interactive features embedded within them such as social media icons, hyperlinks to related articles, one-click donation buttons etc. Try to include these in your text to create an authentic piece.

Option 3: Class debate

Our online world is often a place for diverse views. Some perspectives presented in online texts can be harmful. People use their right to freedom of expression without thinking about the consequences, or perhaps not thinking there are any.

For this task your teacher could organise and help you prepare for a class debate, or you could get into groups to plan and then discuss the following statement. Half the group should argue for the statement and half against.

Consider the following prompt questions and the quotations as you get started on structuring your points.

Some perspectives presented in texts can harm rather than heal, and should be censored by governments.

Read the quotations below to help inform your discussion.

'To uphold the right to gratuitously offend, without any sense of responsibility that should accompany freedom of expression, is childish, even dangerous.' – Sharif Nashashibi

'You can't pick and choose which types of freedom you want to defend. You must defend all of it or be against all of it.' – Scott Howard Phillips

'There's a time and a place for getting a smart mouth.' – JK Rowling

'It is easy to believe in freedom of speech for those with whom we agree.' – Leo McKern

Be guided by the following questions to plan, write and argue in your debate.

- Should the freedoms in our society be expected or earned?
- Who should have the power to remove freedoms?
- How can language cause division and promote harmony?
- Should the same expectations be upheld in online and face-to-face communication?
- Are there countries where censorship is the norm? How does this work?

Assessment as learning: self-assessment

Does my composition ...

- ☐ present a clear perspective?
- ☐ use appropriate structure?
- ☐ experiment with figurative language and devices?
- ☐ craft concise sentences?

What are two strengths of my response?

____

____

What area/s of my response do I need to refine further?

____

____

UNIT 03

Heroes and villains

Unit inquiry question:
How do authors depict heroes and villains in literature and how do these representations evolve over time?

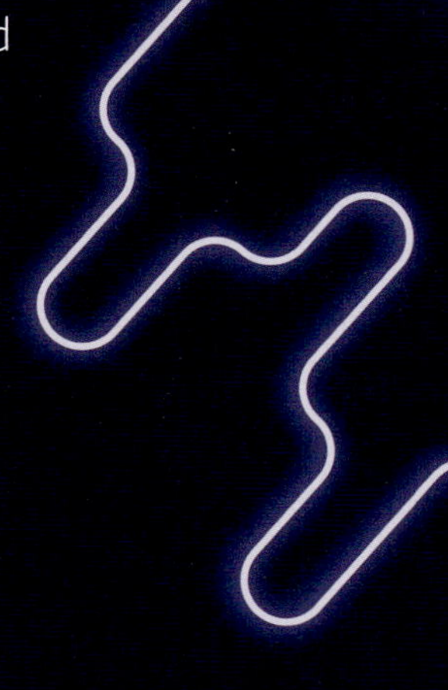

Students will learn about an important and frequently encountered literary tool, the hero's journey. They will explore the inception of the hero's journey, as well as its timeless nature and influence, through analysing its structural components. Students will evaluate the traditional representation of a villain and learn how some authors have challenged these depictions.

This unit has been broken into three chapters, each of which looks at a different aspect of texts and archetypes and raises additional inquiry questions.

Students will have the opportunity to consider everything they have learned about what a hero is to the people in their own nation and local communities. They will be encouraged to work together to research Australian heroes from all walks of life and evaluate why they are considered heroic. Students will collaborate to create spoken, written and visual texts.

Chapter 7
The hero's journey

In this chapter, students will learn about the timeless 'monomyth', the hero's journey. Students will also explore and analyse the codes and conventions of the hero's journey.

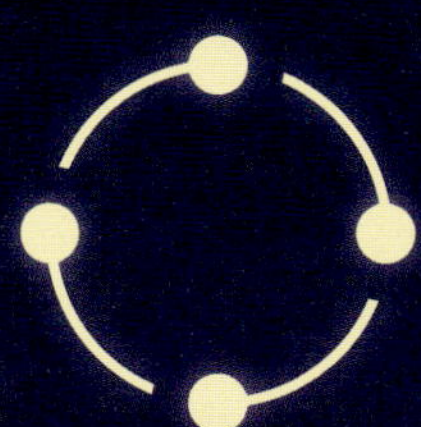

Chapter 8
Determined to prove a villain

In this chapter, students will explore the popular character archetype of the villain. They will examine the common traits of a villain and how these traditional representations have been challenged and subverted.

Chapter 9
Local heroes

In this final chapter, students will consider how ordinary people, particularly Australians, can be extraordinary through selfless acts of heroism and their service to others.

The learning activities within each chapter and the summative assessment options (on page 134) provide opportunities to assess student achievement of the following outcomes:

Outcome and Focus Area	Content point
EN5-RVL-01 Reading, viewing and listening to texts	**Reading, viewing and listening for meaning**
	Analyse the main ideas and thematic concerns represented in texts Analyse how language use evolves over time and is influenced by social and technological changes and developments
	Reading for challenge, interest and enjoyment
	Consider how the social, cultural and ethical positions represented in texts represent, affirm or challenge views of the world Evaluate the ways reading texts help us understand ourselves and make connections to others and the world
	Reflecting
	Understand and reflect on the value of reading for personal growth and cultural richness
EN5-URA-01 Understanding and responding to texts A	**Code and convention**
	Explain how texts use, adapt or subvert textual conventions across a range of modes and media to shape new meanings, and explore this in own texts
	Characterisation
	Analyse how characters can serve structural roles in narrative, such as foils and drivers of action and conflict, and manipulate these ideas when composing own texts
	Narrative
	Explore how narratives can represent and shape personal and shared identities, values and experiences
EN5-URC-01 Understanding and responding to texts C	**Literary value**
	Analyse and evaluate how thematic and aesthetic qualities of a text contribute to the different ways an audience questions and negotiates the value of the text in particular contexts

EN5-ECA-01 Expressing ideas and composing texts A	**Writing**
	Select and adapt appropriate codes, conventions and structures to shape meaning when composing written texts that are analytical, informative, persuasive, discursive and/or imaginative
	Representing
	Experiment with a variety of codes and conventions to create aesthetic qualities that have the power to communicate ideas and influence viewpoints in own texts
	Text features
	Use the structural conventions of analytical writing purposefully, including a well-articulated and considered thesis, a sustained and cohesive progression of supporting points, and a rhetorically effective conclusion Experiment with the process of transformation to create texts with new meaning
	Word-level language
	Select technical vocabulary to write with accuracy in a range of modes and registers appropriate to audience, purpose, form and context
	Speaking
	Deliver spoken, signed or communicated texts with engaging use of intonation, emphasis, volume, pace and timing
EN5-ECB-01 Expressing ideas and composing texts B	**Planning, monitoring and revising**
	Research, summarise, evaluate and synthesise information and perspectives from different sources to generate new ideas and create detailed and informed texts

Chapter 7

THE HERO'S JOURNEY

Chapter overview

In this chapter, you will learn about one of the oldest narrative structures, the hero's journey. You will understand the stages of this journey and how to identify these in texts. You will examine how the hero's journey is a narrative tool and consider the function of some of the key steps.

You will also reflect on the popularity of the hero's journey narrative structure and experiment with using it in your own compositions.

Success criteria: In this chapter, I will be successful when I can ...

- read and understand extracts from prose
- understand and identify the hero's journey
- analyse the narrative structure of the hero's journey in texts
- experiment with using the codes and conventions of the hero's journey in my own compositions
- reflect on the lessons I can learn from heroic narratives.

Chapter inquiry questions

- What is the hero's journey?
- How can we analyse the hero's journey in texts?
- How can I create my own narratives incorporating the elements of the hero's journey?

Key vocabulary

- Narrative
- Monomyth
- Archetype

What is the hero's journey?

'A hero ventures forth from the world of common day into a region of supernatural wonder: fabulous forces are there encountered, and a decisive victory is won: the hero comes back from this mysterious adventure with the power to bestow boons on his fellow man.' – Joseph Campbell

You may have heard about the hero's journey, and you may have some idea of what it refers to. The hero's journey is an excellent way to analyse narratives.

3.7.1 Warm-up

Write the opening to a narrative using this image as your prompt.

Let's take a closer look at how the hero's journey was first conceived.

American writer Joseph Campbell wrote a book called *The Hero with a Thousand Faces*, which records his research into myths and stories from around the world. Campbell discovered that there were many common, organic patterns running through these hero stories. He identified stages that almost all hero narratives subconsciously or consciously followed. This is what Campbell calls 'the monomyth', which is commonly known as the hero's journey.

We can think of the **monomyth** comprising of three basic 'acts' or sections:

Departure: the hero leaves their home to go on a quest.

Initiation: Facing many trials and tribulations, the hero is eventually victorious on their quest.

Return: the hero returns home with gifts and 'boons' (something beneficial).

Here is what Campbell's monomyth looks like following the three-act structure:

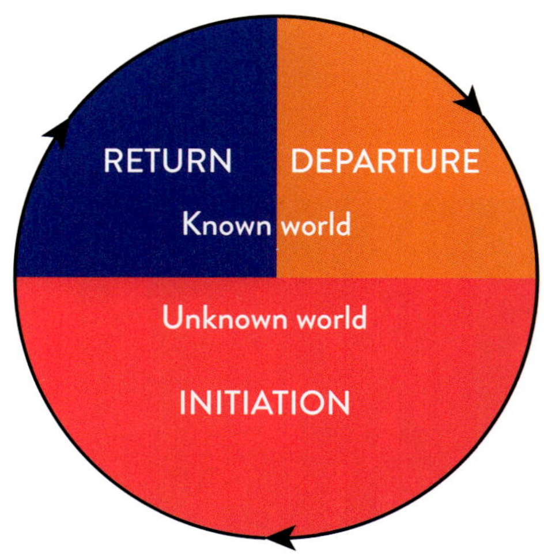

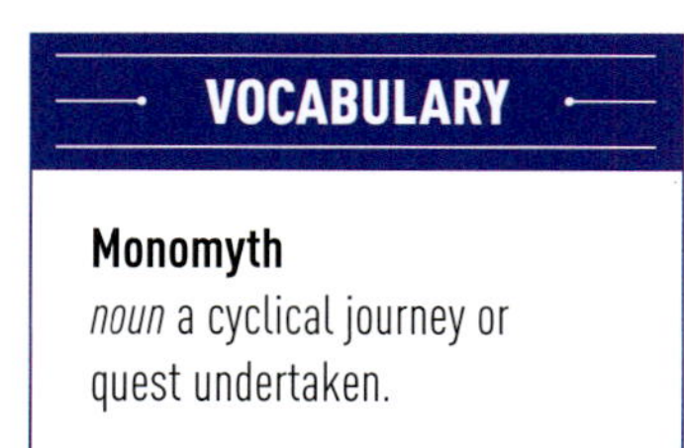

Monomyth
noun a cyclical journey or quest undertaken.

3.7.2 Reading, viewing and listening to texts

Campbell's monomyth has been transformed into twelve steps. Look at the diagram:

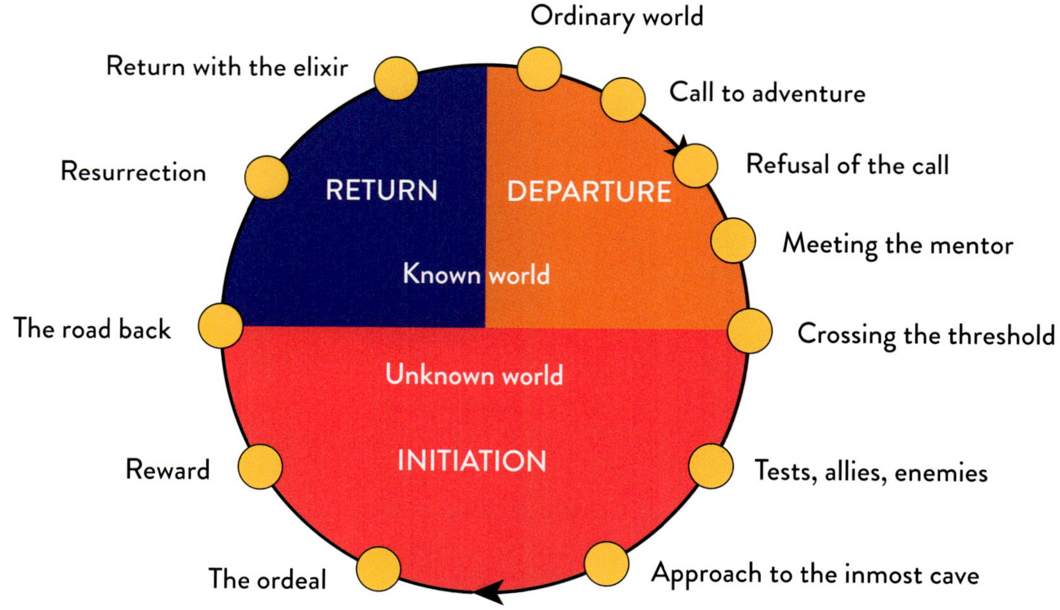

Discuss with a partner what you notice about these twelve steps. Can you think of examples of these steps from a book or film?

How can we analyse the hero's journey in texts?

The hero's journey is essentially a physical journey of a 'hero' who undergoes great psychological growth and change. Through overcoming obstacles and defeating 'monsters', the **protagonist** is transformed to a higher self, experiencing psychological healing and spiritual growth.

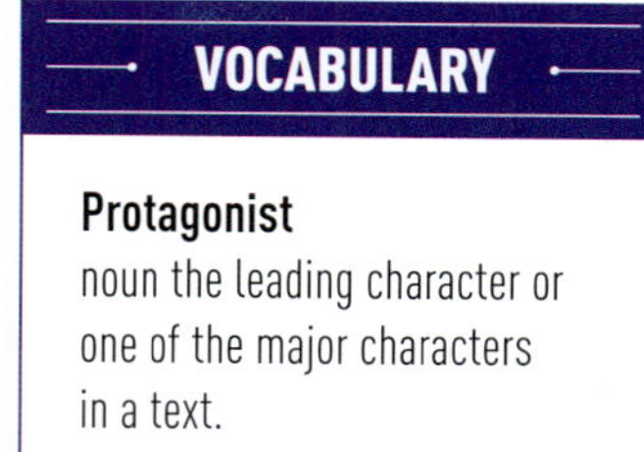

VOCABULARY

Protagonist
noun the leading character or one of the major characters in a text.

3.7.3 Understanding and responding to texts A

Let's take a closer look at the three stages of the hero's journey and examine some of the key steps. To help you understand the stages, you will read extracts from *The Hunger Games*.

Scan the QR code or research online to read a summary of The Hunger Games *if you want to learn more.*

1 Departure

The ordinary world

The opening of the monomyth is designed to present to us the hero's ordinary, simple and mundane life. The hero is also fairly ordinary, but they have hidden traits that make them take a stand and rise to the call to adventure.

Read the extract from The Hunger Games. *Here, we meet our hero, Katniss.*

1 Underline the aspects of this extract that reflect the ordinary world.

I prop myself up on one elbow. There's enough light in the bedroom to see them. My little sister, Prim, curled up on her side, cocooned in my mother's body, their cheeks pressed together. In sleep, my mother looks younger, still worn but not so beaten-down. Prim's face is as fresh as a raindrop, as lovely as the primrose for which she was named. My mother was very beautiful once, too. Or so they tell me ...

Our part of District 12, nicknamed the Seam, is usually crawling with coal miners heading out to the morning shift at this hour. Men and women with hunched shoulders, swollen knuckles, many who have long since stopped trying to scrub the coal dust out of their broken nails, the lines of their sunken faces. But today the black cinder streets are empty. Shutters on the squat gray houses are closed. The reaping isn't until two. May as well sleep in. If you can.

Our house is almost at the edge of the Seam. I only have to pass a few gates to reach the scruffy field called the Meadow. Separating the Meadow from the woods, in fact enclosing all of District 12, is a high chain-link fence topped with barbed-wire loops. In theory, it's supposed to be electrified twenty-four hours a day as a deterrent to the predators that live in the woods – packs of wild dogs, lone cougars, bears – that used to threaten our streets. But since we're lucky to get two or three hours of electricity in the evenings, it's usually safe to touch. Even so, I always take a moment to listen carefully for the hum that means the fence is live. Right now, it's silent as a stone. Concealed by a clump of bushes, I flatten out on my belly and slide under a two-foot stretch that's been loose for years. There are several other weak spots in the fence, but this one is so close to home I almost always enter the woods here.

As soon as I'm in the trees, I retrieve a bow and sheath of arrows from a hollow log. Electrified or not, the fence has been successful at keeping the flesh-eaters out of District 12. Inside the woods they roam freely, and there are added concerns like venomous snakes, rabid animals, and no real paths to follow. But there's also food if you know how to find it. My father knew and he taught me some before he was blown to bits in a mine explosion.

2 **Explain why you think that the reader needs to see the hero in their ordinary world.**

The call to adventure

Let's look at the next step of the hero's journey, the call to adventure. In this stage, the hero is made aware of a danger or need in their community. This may be an existing situation, or they may be directly asked to embark on a journey. Either way, the 'call' is what pushes the hero out of their comfortable and known world.

Read the extract from The Hunger Games.

3 **Underline the aspects of this extract that reflect Katniss's call to adventure.**

It's time for the drawing. Effie Trinket says as she always does, 'Ladies first!' and crosses to the glass ball with the girls' names. She reaches in, digs her hand deep into the ball, and pulls out a slip of paper. The crowd draws in a collective breath and then you can hear a pin drop, and I'm feeling nauseous and so desperately hoping that it's not me, that it's not me, that it's not me.

Effie Trinket crosses back to the podium, smooths the slip of paper, and reads out the name in a clear voice. And it's not me.

It's Primrose Everdeen.

... 'Prim!' The strangled cry comes out of my throat, and my muscles begin to move again. 'Prim!' I don't need to shove through the crowd. The other kids make way immediately allowing me a straight path to the stage. I reach her just as she is about to mount the steps. With one sweep of my arm, I push her behind me.

'I volunteer!' I gasp. 'I volunteer as tribute!'

4 In this extract, we learn that Katniss's little sister Primrose is chosen at the reaping to be the tribute for the Hunger Games – facing almost certain death. Here, the 'call' comes through a situation. Explain what the call is here and what compels Katniss to respond.

5 Explain why the call to adventure is a necessary part of the hero's journey. What does it help the audience learn?

2 Initiation

Let's look at the 'initiation' stage of the hero's journey, where the hero enters the 'unknown' world. One of the most important steps in this stage is the ordeal.

The ordeal

In the ordeal stage, many things go wrong for the hero and further conflict is introduced. The hero endures more challenging hurdles and obstacles, and there is a nearly impossible task that the hero must accomplish to fulfill their goal. The ordeal is a test of strength, strategy and skill. In the ordeal, the hero will achieve their goal, but their journey is not over.

Read the extract from The Hunger Games. *Here, Katniss and the other tributes enter the arena and must learn how to survive, or they will die.*

6 Underline the aspects of this extract that reflect the ordeal.

Sixty seconds. That's how long we're required to stand on our metal circles before the sound of a gong releases us. Step off before the minute is up, and land mines blow your legs off. Sixty seconds to take in the ring of tributes all equidistant from the Cornucopia, a giant golden horn shaped like a cone with a curved tail, the mouth of which is at least twenty feet high, spilling over with the things that will give us life here in the arena. Food, containers of water, weapons, medicine, garments, fire starters. ... But there in the mouth, I can see a tent pack that would protect from almost any sort of weather. If I had the guts to go in and fight for it against the other twenty-three tributes. Which I have been instructed not to do. ...

It's late afternoon when I begin to hear the cannons. Each shot represents a dead tribute ... On the opening day, they don't even fire the cannons until the initial fighting's over because it's too hard to keep track of the fatalities. I allow myself to pause, panting, as I count the shots. One ... two ... three ... on and on until they reach eleven. Eleven dead in all. Thirteen left to play. ... I wonder about Peeta. Has he lasted through the day? I'll know in a few hours. When they project the dead's images into the sky for the rest of us to see. ...

What I want most, right at this moment, is water. Haymitch's directive to immediately find water was not arbitrary. I won't last long without it. ...

I become aware of the dryness in my throat and mouth, the cracks in my lips. ...

As I refill my pack I have an awful thought. The lake. ... The lake is a full day's journey from where I sit now, a much harder journey with nothing to drink. And then, even if I reach it, it's sure to be heavily guarded ... I'm about to panic when I remember the rabbit I startled earlier today. It has to drink, too. I just have to find out where. ...

But by afternoon, I know the end is coming. My legs are shaking and my heart too quick. I keep forgetting, exactly what I'm doing. I've stumbled repeatedly and managed to regain my feet, but when the stick slides out from under me, I finally tumble to the ground unable to get up. I let my eyes close. ...

A few hours later, the stampede of feet shakes me from slumber. I look around in bewilderment. It's not yet dawn, but my stinging eyes can see it.

It would be hard to miss the wall of fire descending on me. ...

My leg is in need of attention, but I still can't look at it ... Then I remember my mother saying that if a burn's severe, the victim might not even feel pain because the nerves would be destroyed. Encouraged by this, I sit up and swing my leg in front of me.

I almost faint at the sight of my calf. The flesh is a brilliant red covered with blisters. I force myself to take deep, slow breaths, feeling quite certain the cameras are on my face. I can't show weakness at this injury. Not if I want help. Pity does not get you aid. Admiration at your refusal to give in does.

7 Explain how Katniss is tested in the ordeal step.

___

___

3 Return

Let's look at the 'return' stage of the hero's journey where the hero re-enters the known world.

The return with the elixir

This step is when we come to the end of the journey. The hero returns triumphant, but more importantly, they return bringing life, purpose and hope back into their world. Traditionally, the elixir is a medicine or potion, but it can also represent anything that brings healing (physically, spiritually or emotionally) to the community. It can also be something that brings a renewed or restored way of doing or thinking.

Read the extract from The Hunger Games. *Here, Katniss has beaten the Gamemakers by making them declare her and Peeta as dual victors. She is crowned and applauded, but there are hints that she will need to pay for what she's done.*

Blinding lights. The deafening roar rattles the metal under my feet. Then there's Peeta just a few yards away. He looks so clean and healthy and beautiful, I can hardly recognise him. But his smile is the same whether in mud or in the Capitol and when I see it, I take about three steps and fling myself into his arms. He staggers back, almost losing his balance, and that's when I realize the slim, metal contraption in his hand is some kind of cane. He rights himself and we just cling to each other while the audience goes insane. He's kissing me and all the time I'm thinking, Do you know? Do you know how much danger we're in? After about ten minutes of this, Caesar Flickerman taps on his shoulder to continue the show, and Peeta just pushes him aside without even glancing at him. The audience goes berserk. Whether he knows or not, Peeta is, as usual, playing the crowd exactly right.

8 What do you think is the elixir that Katniss brings?

____

____

3.7.4 Expressing ideas and composing texts A and B

Write a paragraph explaining how *The Hunger Games* follows the hero's journey. Remember to start your paragraph with a topic sentence that introduces your argument, include supporting points and use evidence from the extracts to illustrate your argument.

____

____

____

____

____

____

____

____

Read the following quotation:

> 'Does every play have to follow this structure? Of course not, but for plays that do, it's the key to knowing what a character wants and why the audience should care. We like when characters change, we like when they transform as people – that's what keeps the audience invested. The audience buys tickets because of the first half of a play; they stay because of the second half.' – David Lindsay-Abaire

Think about why the hero's journey is so popular. Discuss your ideas with a partner and explain what you think are the reasons for the timeless qualities of this narrative structure. Share with the class.

Extension activity

Choose a hero from Greek mythology like Hercules, Jason, Odysseus, Perseus or Theseus. Read about their journey and identify twelve steps to determine how it follows the monomyth. Choose one of the steps and write a descriptive paragraph (in a separate notebook) about this moment in the journey from the perspective of the hero.

How can I create my own narratives incorporating the elements of the hero's journey?

3.7.5 Expressing ideas and composing texts A

Write your own hero's journey using the three essential stages: the departure, initiation and return.

1 Firstly, use the following template to plan your journey:

	What happens?	
Departure	What's the adventure?	
Initiation	What lesson is learned? What victory do they win?	

Return	How has the hero been transformed? What 'elixir' do they bring?	

2 Then, write your hero's journey. Discuss with your teacher whether to write the whole narrative, or just one of the stages.

3.7.6 Chapter reflection

1 I enjoyed learning about the hero's journey because ...

2 In this chapter, the activity that I liked the most was

because ...

3 What is the hero's journey? Create a mind-map outlining what you have learned about the hero's journey. Include ideas about how you would define the narrative structure.

4 Outline the stories you're aware of that follow the hero's journey structure.

5 The hero's journey narrative is a popular form of storytelling. Partly this is due to how the narrative structure can teach us about human nature and some important life lessons (e.g. resilience, perseverance, sacrifice, etc.). What do you think are some lessons you can learn from the hero's journey?

6 Let's return to the unit inquiry question: ***How do authors depict heroes and villains in literature and how do these representations evolve over time?*** How have your reading experiences in this chapter addressed this inquiry question?

CHAPTER 8

DETERMINED TO PROVE A VILLAIN

Chapter overview

In this chapter, you will examine how authors represent villainy. You will evaluate the traditional representation of a villain and learn how some authors have challenged these depictions to add complexity and depth to their villains. Over the last hundred years, we have seen the depiction of heroes and villains change, reflecting changes in values, the way we tell stories, and the expectations of the audience. You will consider the changing nature of villains and experiment with your own interpretation and characterisation of the villain.

Success criteria: In this chapter, I will be successful when I can ...

- read, view and understand extracts from a variety of modes and media
- understand and identify the traits of a villain
- analyse how texts use, adapt or subvert textual conventions to shape new ideas of the villain, and experiment with this in my own compositions
- analyse how villains can serve structural roles in narratives and manipulate these ideas when composing my own texts
- experiment with using the codes and conventions of the hero's journey in my own compositions
- select and adapt appropriate codes, conventions and structures to shape meaning when composing written texts.

Chapter inquiry questions

- What makes a villain?
- How do authors challenge traditional notions of villainy?
- How have interpretations of villains evolved over time?

Key vocabulary

- Villain
- Archetype
- Antagonist
- Antihero

Villains

In the previous chapter, we learned a little about the hero through looking at the hero's journey. Stories need heroes. Heroes give the reader a platform from which to view the story and a champion for whom to cheer. But, without the villain, how does the hero grow and how do we know that the hero is *heroic*? The villain is essential as they provide the conflict and are often the obstacle that stops the hero from getting what they want. This is what many writers understand – good stories have great conflict, and great conflict comes from evil, greedy, brutal and manipulative villains.

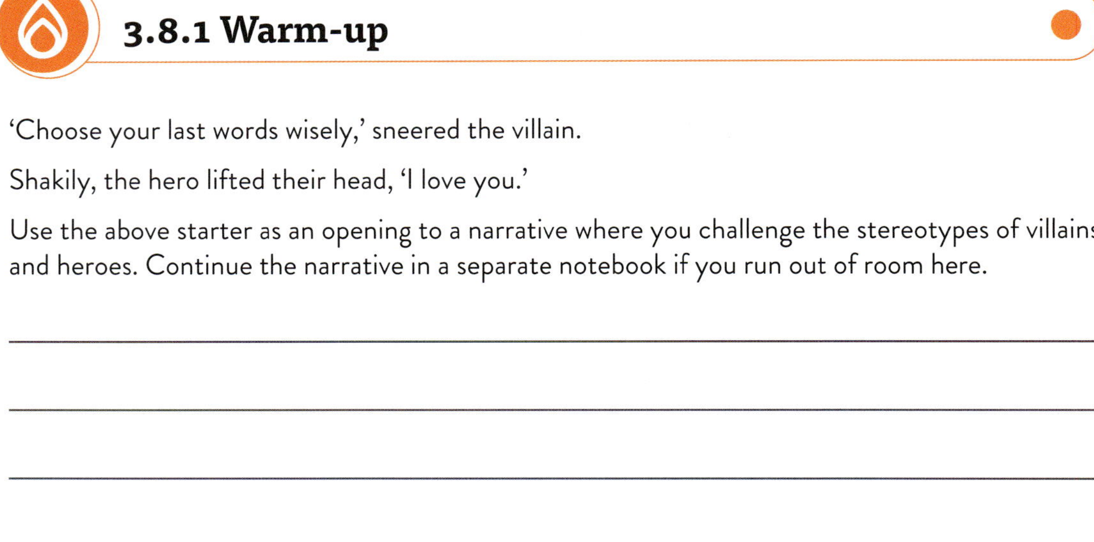

3.8.1 Warm-up

'Choose your last words wisely,' sneered the villain.

Shakily, the hero lifted their head, 'I love you.'

Use the above starter as an opening to a narrative where you challenge the stereotypes of villains and heroes. Continue the narrative in a separate notebook if you run out of room here.

What makes a villain?

Most of us have grown up reading and viewing stories that entertain us with the fight for good over evil. The hero inevitably triumphs over the villain. Good wins out. We cheer the hero, our champion, and we enjoy seeing the villain fail.

3.8.2 Reading, viewing and listening to texts

Look at these images of villains.

What are the first words that come to mind when you think about the word 'villain'? What should a villain be like? Brainstorm your ideas in the space below.

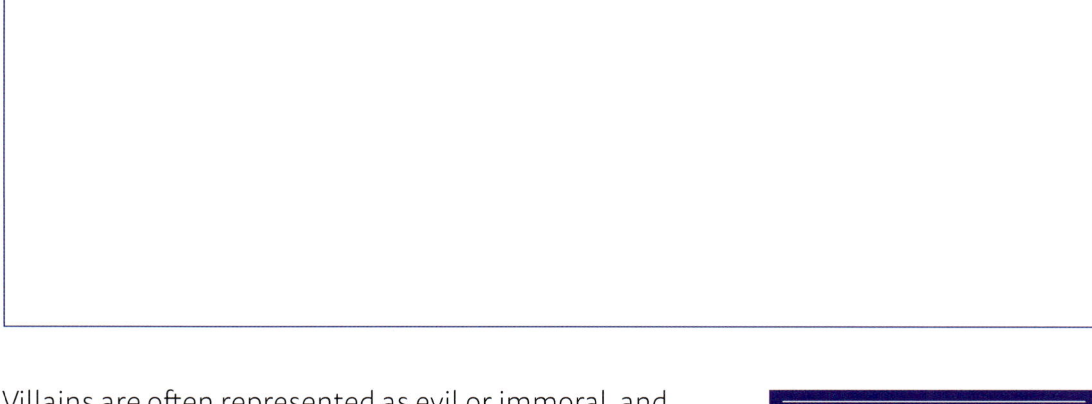

Villains are often represented as evil or immoral, and indifferent to the pain of others. We interpret the villain in contrast to the hero. The villain is selfish, where the hero is selfless; greedy as opposed to generous; proud rather than humble. Villains are the **antagonist**, the typical 'bad person'. Some of the most well-known villains are Lord Voldemort, Cruella de Vil, Darth Vader, Count Dracula and the Joker.

It's important for you to understand that there are common character archetypes in literature. Heroes and villains are the most common examples of **archetypes**. Even though heroes and villains appear in different modes and mediums, their traits are universal.

VOCABULARY

Antagonist
noun a person who actively goes against or is hostile to someone or something.

LANGUAGE

Archetype
What is an *archetype?*
An archetype is a typical example of a certain person or thing. In narratives, characters are created based on specific traits that make them easily identifiable for readers, and these recur from story to story.

3.8.3 Reading, viewing and listening to texts

Villains come in all sorts of shapes and sizes. Let's have a look at three different types.

1 Look at the table headings and associated images. For each type of villain, brainstorm examples of characters from myths, poems, video games, books, films and TV shows.

The Trickster	The Evil Overlord	The Heartless Manipulator

2 Compare your examples to a partner's. Are there similarities or differences? Discuss.

3 Conduct some research into each villain type. Write a paragraph for two of the villain types, outlining their main traits, what motivates them and their function. The first one has been done for you.

The Trickster	The Evil Overlord	The Heartless Manipulator
Relying on cleverness and manipulation, the trickster villain uses their intelligence, deception and cunning to achieve their goals. They just want everyone to know that they are brilliant and superior to the hero. Sometimes, they also want something, usually from the hero. These bad characters are driven by greed or jealousy and will do whatever it takes to get what they want.		

3.8.3 Understanding and responding to texts A

Let's have a look at some famous villains from film and literature. For each villain, study both the visual and written representation to examine how visual and language choices are being used.

SAURON

DISCUSS

Discuss how, in this image of Sauron, his body language communicates power.

IDENTIFY

Identify the **salient** feature of this film still. Think about what it suggests about the traits of this villain.

The Return of the King

By J.R.R. Tolkien

And far away, as Frodo put on the Ring and claimed it for his own, even in Sammath Naur the very heart of his realm, the Power in **Barad-dûr** was shaken, and the Tower trembled from its foundations to its proud and bitter crown. The Dark Lord was suddenly aware of him, and his Eye piercing all shadows looked across the plain to the door that he had made; and the magnitude of his own folly was revealed to him in a blinding flash, and all the devices of his enemies were at last laid bare. Then his wrath blazed in consuming flame, but his fear rose like a vast black smoke to choke him. For he knew his deadly peril and the thread upon which his doom now hung.

From all his policies and webs of fear and treachery, from all his stratagems and wars his mind shook free; and throughout his realm a tremor ran, his slaves quailed, and his armies halted, and his captains suddenly steerless, bereft of will, wavered and despaired. For they were forgotten. The whole mind and purpose of the Power that wielded them was now bent with overwhelming force upon the Mountain. At his summons, wheeling with a rending cry, in a last desperate race there flew, faster than the winds, the **Nazgûl**, the Ringwraiths, and with a storm of wings they hurtled southwards to Mount Doom.

This extract is depicting the moment when Frodo (the hero) puts on the Ring, claiming it for himself, which triggers this reaction in Sauron's realm.

Barad-dûr was a tower built by Sauron as his 'base of operations' in Mordor.

IDENTIFY

Underline the verbs used for Sauron in paragraph one.

IDENTIFY

Circle the nouns used for Sauron in paragraph two.

Nazgûl were Sauron's servants. The Ring made them invisible and enslaved them to Sauron.

1 Which villainous traits are being communicated by both the film still and the extract about Sauron?

2 What type of villain is Sauron? Justify your opinion with two examples.

LOKI

DISCUSS

Discuss what villainous traits are being communicated in this book cover.

INTERPRET

Discuss what you think the green mist suggests about Loki.

IDENTIFY

Circle the part of Loki's body language that communicates a 'Trickster Villain' trait.

THINK

Think about the symbolic nature of colour. What could green be suggesting about Loki?

The Gospel of Loki

By Joanne M. Harris

'Er, hi,' I said. 'I know it must seem strange to you that someone like me should want to hang out with people like you. But give me a chance and I'll prove to you I'm not a spy. I swear it. I've burnt my boats by coming here; I'm a traitor to my people. Send me back, and they'll kill me – or worse.'

'So?' That was Heimdall, a flashy type, with golden armour and teeth to match. 'We don't need a traitor's help. Treachery's a crooked rune that never flies straight, or hits the mark.'

IDENTIFY

Underline examples of Loki's traits and label which trait it is suggesting. An example has been provided in the first paragraph.

Intelligence and manipulation.

That was typical Heimdall, or so I came to realize later. Pompous, rude, and arrogant. His rune was Madr, straight as a die, boxy and pedestrian. I thought of the mark of Kaen on my arm and said:

'Sometimes crooked is better than straight.'

'You think so?' said Heimdall.

'Let's try it,' I said. 'My glam against yours. Let Odin decide the victor.'

There was an archery target outside. I'd noticed it as we came in. The gods were predictably keen on sports; popular types so often are. I'd never used a bow before, but I understood the principle.

'Come on, Goldie,' I said, and grinned. 'Or are you having second thoughts?'

'I'll give you this,' he said. 'You can talk. Now let's see how well you perform.'

Aesir and Vanir followed us out. Odin came last, looking curious. 'Heimdall's the best shot in Asgard,' he said. 'The Vanir call him Hawkeye.'

I shrugged. 'So what?'

'So you'd better be good.'

I grinned again. 'I'm Loki,' I said. 'Good doesn't enter into it.'

We stood in front of the target. I could tell from his colours that Heimdall was sure of beating me; his golden smile radiated confidence. Behind him, all the rest of them stared at me with suspicion and scorn. I'd thought that I knew prejudice, but this lot redefined it. I could see them itching to spill some of my demon blood, even though it ran through the veins of a dozen or more of them. Heimdall himself was one of them ... but I could see he wasn't about to celebrate our kinship. There are races that hate each other on sight – mongoose and snake, cat and dog – and though I didn't know much of the Worlds, I guessed that the straightforward, muscular type would be the natural enemy of the lithe and devious type who thinks with his head and not his fists.

DISCUSS

Discuss with a partner what you think Loki's narrative 'voice' is like. How does it sound?

DISCUSS

This last paragraph demonstrates Loki's ability to understand people and how they think. Discuss why you think this is an important trait for a villain.

1. Explain how Loki is different from Sauron.

___

___

2. What similarities and differences can you find between how the book cover and the extract have represented Loki? (Note that the cover and the extract are different books).

Similarities	Differences

LADY MACBETH

INTERPRET

Discuss what sort of villain you think Lady Macbeth could be based just on the composition of this poster.

IDENTIFY

Circle the part of Lady Macbeth's body language that is suggesting power or ambition.

IDENTIFY

In Unit 1, Chapter 3, you learned about gaze. Label the type of gaze and write down its effect.

Macbeth

By William Shakespeare

LADY MACBETH
The **raven** himself is hoarse
That croaks the **fatal** entrance of Duncan
Under my battlements. Come, **you spirits**
That tend on mortal thoughts, unsex me here,

IDENTIFY

Underline each thing that Lady Macbeth is asking the 'spirits' to do to her (*hint* – follow the punctuation and pay attention to the verbs).

INTERPRET

Symbolism: Ravens are ill-omens and were seen as heralds of misfortune or death. Discuss why the raven's cry is 'hoarse'.

Mortal thoughts are deadly thoughts (i.e. thoughts of murder).

And fill me from the crown to the toe top-full
Of direst cruelty! make thick my blood;
Stop up the access and passage to remorse,
That no compunctious visitings of nature
Shake my fell purpose, nor keep peace between
The effect and it! Come to my woman's breasts,
And take my milk for gall, **you murdering ministers**,
Wherever in your sightless substances
You wait on nature's mischief! Come, thick night,
And pall thee in the dunnest smoke of hell,
That my keen knife see not the wound it makes,
Nor heaven peep through the blanket of the dark,
To cry 'Hold, hold!'

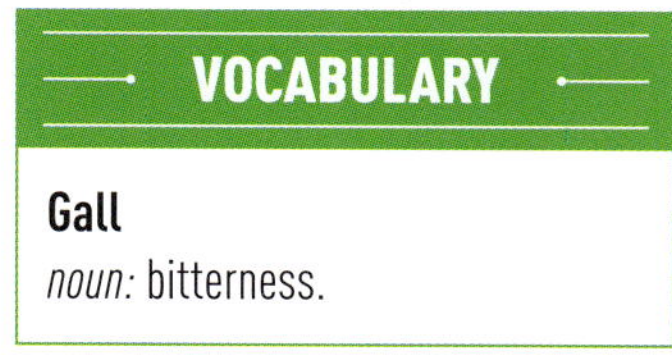

Gall
noun: bitterness.

DISCUSS

Discuss with a partner why you think she is asking this? What's her motivation?

DISCUSS

Discuss with a partner what type of villain you think Lady Macbeth is.

IDENTIFY

Circle the word 'come'. Think about what the **repetition** is communicating to us about Lady Macbeth's traits.

1 Which villainous traits are being communicated by both the image and the extract about Lady Macbeth?

2 Is Lady Macbeth a villain? Justify your opinion with two examples.

How do authors challenge traditional notions of villainy?

In a lot of stories, the villain represents pure evil, and in the past they have been characterised in a relatively one-dimensional way. They are bad because they are bad. However, some authors have challenged these traditional notions of villainy to add complexity and depth to their characters. The film *Black Panther* presents the villain Killmonger with motivations and a background to evoke sympathy. Likewise, the novel and Broadway musical *Wicked* reimagines the story of *The Wizard of Oz* from the point of view of the Wicked Witch of the West, and the traditional portrayal of the witch as an evil character is challenged.

We are going to learn about how another author challenges the traditional notion of the witch as a villain.

3.8.4 Understanding and responding to texts A

Before we look at how the traditional view of the witch has been challenged, read the following scene extract from Shakespeare's *Macbeth* to understand what a traditional representation may look like.

THE WITCHES

Macbeth

By William Shakespeare

FIRST WITCH
When shall we three meet again –
In thunder, lightning, or in rain?

SECOND WITCH
When the hurlyburly's done,
When the battle's lost, and won.

THIRD WITCH
That will be ere the set of sun.

FIRST WITCH
Where the place?

SECOND WITCH
Upon the heath.

THIRD WITCH
There to meet with Macbeth ...

ALL
Fair is foul, and foul is fair.
Hover through the fog and filthy air.
[Exit]

IDENTIFY

Circle the words and phrases that seem to contradict.

DISCUSS

Discuss what you think is the symbolic meaning of thunder, lightning and rain?

DISCUSS

Discuss what you think 'hurly-burly' means.

DISCUSS

Discuss with a partner what type of villain you think the witches could be.

IDENTIFY

Underline where you see what the witches plan to do. What could this suggest about the nature of their villainy?

What type of villain are the witches and how is Shakespeare presenting this?

____

____

____

Let's read an extract from English humourist Terry Pratchett's fantasy novel *Wyrd Sisters* (1988). Pratchett is explicitly taking the witches from *Macbeth* and challenging the stereotype of the villain.

Pratchett uses humour, satire and fantasy elements to create a witty social commentary and to explore the themes of fate, power and the nature of storytelling. *Wyrd Sisters* also presents an entertaining and rather unique perspective on fairy tales and Shakespearean plays.

Wyrd Sisters

By Terry Pratchett

The wind howled. Lightning stabbed at the earth erratically, like an inefficient assassin. Thunder rolled back and forth across the dark, rain-lashed hills.

The night was as black as the inside of a cat. It was the kind of night, you could believe, on which gods moved men as though they were pawns on the chessboard of fate. In the middle of this elemental storm a fire gleamed among the dripping furze bushes like the madness in a weasel's eye. It illuminated three hunched figures. As the cauldron bubbled an **eldritch** voice shrieked: 'When shall we three meet again?'

There was a pause.

Finally another voice said, in far more ordinary tones: 'Well, I can do next Tuesday.'

...

On nights such as this, witches are abroad. Well, not actually abroad. They don't like the food and you can't trust the water and the shamans always hog the deckchairs. But there was a full moon breasting the ragged clouds and the rushing air was full of whispers and the very broad hint of magic. In their clearing above the forest the witches spoke thus: 'I'm babysitting on Tuesday,' said the one with no hat but a thatch of white curls so thick she might have been wearing a helmet. 'For our Jason's youngest. I can manage Friday. Hurry up with the tea, luv. I'm that parched.' The junior member of the trio gave a sigh, and ladled some boiling water out of the cauldron into the teapot. The third witch patted her hand in a kindly fashion. 'You said it quite well,' she said. 'Just a bit more work on the screeching. Ain't that right, Nanny Ogg?' 'Very useful screeching, I thought,' said Nanny Ogg hurriedly. 'And I can see Goodie Whemper, maysherestinpeace, gave you a lot of help with the squint.' 'It's a good squint,' said

OUT BOX

In this extract we meet three witches: Granny Weatherwax, Nanny Ogg and junior witch, Magrat Garlick.

VOCABULARY

Eldritch
adjective: eerie; weird; spooky.

IDENTIFY

In this description of the tempest, Pratchett is creating a very stereotypical setting to introduce his witches. As you can see, Pratchett is building a scene based on our expectations associated with witches and villainy. Directly after this line, Pratchett subverts our expectations.

Highlight examples of where Pratchett challenges the villain stereotype.

IDENTIFY

Underline the words spoken by the witches that are not what we expect villains to say.

Granny Weatherwax. The junior witch, whose name was Magrat Garlick, relaxed considerably. She held Granny Weatherwax in awe. It was known throughout the Ramtop Mountains that Mss Weatherwax did not approve of anything very much. If she said it was a good squint, then Magrat's eyes were probably staring up her own nostrils. Unlike wizards, who like nothing better than a complicated hierarchy, witches don't go in much for the structured approach to career progression. It's up to each individual witch to take on a girl to hand the area over to when she dies. Witches are not by nature **gregarious**, at least with other witches, and they certainly don't have leaders. Granny Weatherwax was the most highly-regarded of the leaders they didn't have. Magrat's hands shook slightly as they made the tea. Of course, it was all very gratifying, but it was a bit nerve-racking to start one's working life as village witch between Granny and, on the other side of the forest, Nanny Ogg. It'd been her idea to form a local coven. She felt it was more, well, occult. To her amazement the other two had agreed or, at least, hadn't disagreed much. 'An oven?' Nanny Ogg had said. 'What'd we want to join an oven for?' 'She means a coven, Gytha,' Granny Weatherwax had explained. 'You know, like in the old days. A meeting.'

'A knees up?' said Nanny Ogg hopefully.

'No dancing,' Granny had warned. 'I don't hold with dancing. Or singing or getting overexcited or all that messing about with ointments and similar.'

'Does you good to get out,' said Nanny happily.

Magrat had been disappointed about the dancing, and was relieved that she hadn't ventured one or two other ideas that had been on her mind. She fumbled in the packet she had brought with her. It was her first sabbat, and she was determined to do it right.

'Would anyone care for a scone?' she said.

Granny looked hard at hers before she bit. Magrat had baked bat designs on it. They had little eyes made of currants.

VOCABULARY

Gregarious
adjective: sociable.

4.8.5 Understanding and responding to texts A and C

1 Pratchett challenges traditional notions of villains by playing with our expectations of witches. For example, 'I'm babysitting on Tuesday.' We don't expect a witch to say something so ordinary. Find another example and explain what you think Pratchett is suggesting about these witches. What are they really like?

2 If an author reimagines and 'plays around' with traditional characterisations and storytelling, does this mean that the newer text is unoriginal and not as significant? Discuss this with a peer and record your ideas below.

Extension activity

Research Shakespeare's play *Macbeth* and learn more about Act 1, Scene 1. Explain how the opening of *Wyrd Sisters* is satirising the play and other common images of witches. What do you think is Pratchett's purpose in doing this?

How have interpretations of villains evolved over time?

Modern audiences demand a little more from their villains than audiences of the past, as they are not so accepting of the simple binaries of good and evil. The world has become more interested in the shades of grey in human psychology, the motivations, desires and reasons for human behaviour.

> **'The lines between hero and villains can be blurred when villains show themselves to be capable of having heroic characteristics. When the villains have some random acts of goodness, it throws off the audience and readers and creates a form of suspense.'**
> **– Marilyn Horowitz**

More and more, audiences are wanting to relate to the villain and understand their perspective, like Tom Hiddleston (actor who portrayed Loki) points out, 'Well, I think there are no villains in this world. There are just misunderstood heroes.' A great example of this is Darth Vader from *Star Wars*. In the first three films that were released, we were presented with a very one-dimensional Darth Vader, but the subsequent films have provided the audience with the backstory of Anakin Skywalker, where we learn about how he became Darth Vader and why. We see Darth Vader from a new perspective.

Severus Snape from *Harry Potter* is another great example. He is morally ambiguous, and, like Darth Vader, he has a complicated past. At times, Snape is perceived as a true villain who creates conflict and gets in the way of Harry achieving his goals. However, at other times, JK Rowling shows us a softer side to Snape, where he is loyal and conflicted. So, is he good or bad? This is where we have the formation of the **antihero**.

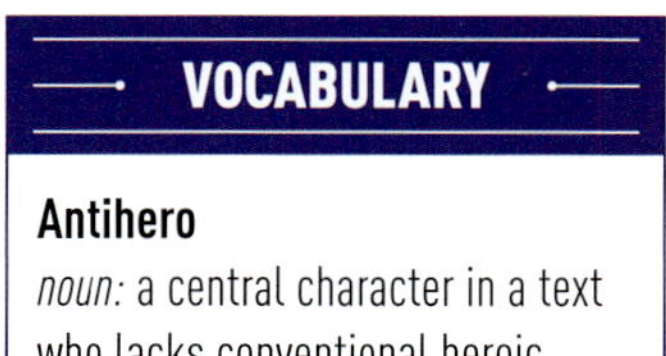

VOCABULARY

Antihero
noun: a central character in a text who lacks conventional heroic attributes.

3.8.6 Expressing ideas and composing texts A and B

1 Choose a villain or an antihero (from a text or your own creation). In a separate notebook, write a character profile. Include information like their physical appearance, past, family, relationships, qualities, flaws and traits. Also include their motivation: what do they want?

2 The villain's journey. In Chapter 7, you learned about the hero's journey. Recreate the hero's journey diagram to adapt it for a villain or antihero. Incorporate the same idea of three stages and twelve steps but change the labels.

3 Write a short scene in which you place your villain or antihero in a situation that forces your character to question their beliefs or motivations. Use your character profile to help you create a genuine and interesting villain.

Extension activity

Research a famous villain, like the Joker, and track how representations of this villain have changed over time. Choose three to five representations. Can you explain how each representation reflects a change in context? Discuss as a class.

3.8.7 Chapter reflection

Let's return to the unit inquiry question: ***How do authors depict heroes and villains in literature and how do these representations evolve over time?***

1 In this chapter, you have been presented with a variety of representations of the villain. Summarise these in the table.

Villain	What is the villain like?
Sauron	
Loki	
Lady Macbeth	
Wyrd Sisters	

2. How did reading the texts in this chapter influence your understanding of villains?

CHAPTER 9

LOCAL HEROES

Chapter overview

In this chapter, you will be invited to think about what makes an everyday hero. Without the superpowers of a Marvel or DC character, can someone closer to home transform lives and be an inspiration?

Success criteria: In this chapter, I will be successful when I can ...

- analyse the main ideas and thematic concerns represented in texts
- evaluate the ways texts help us understand ourselves and make connections to others and the world
- synthesise information from a range of sources to create a variety of texts
- devise open-ended questions to engage an audience in an interview scenario
- reflect on the qualities of heroes and recognise these qualities in the people around me.

Chapter inquiry questions

- Are heroes born or made?
- Are there any real-life heroes in our communities?
- Who are your local heroes?

Key vocabulary

- Flashback
- Ellipsis
- Open-ended questions

Are heroes born or made?

Throughout history, heroes have been a large part of stories and cultures. In Chapter 7, you learned about the hero by studying the narrative structure known as the hero's journey. In these narratives, the hero is represented as having courage, amazing skills and admirable qualities. Some authors suggest that these heroes are special, should be positioned slightly above the ordinary person and are born with these qualities. However, there are other views that argue that a hero does not have to be born 'special', but they can become a hero through overcoming their fears to do good for others.

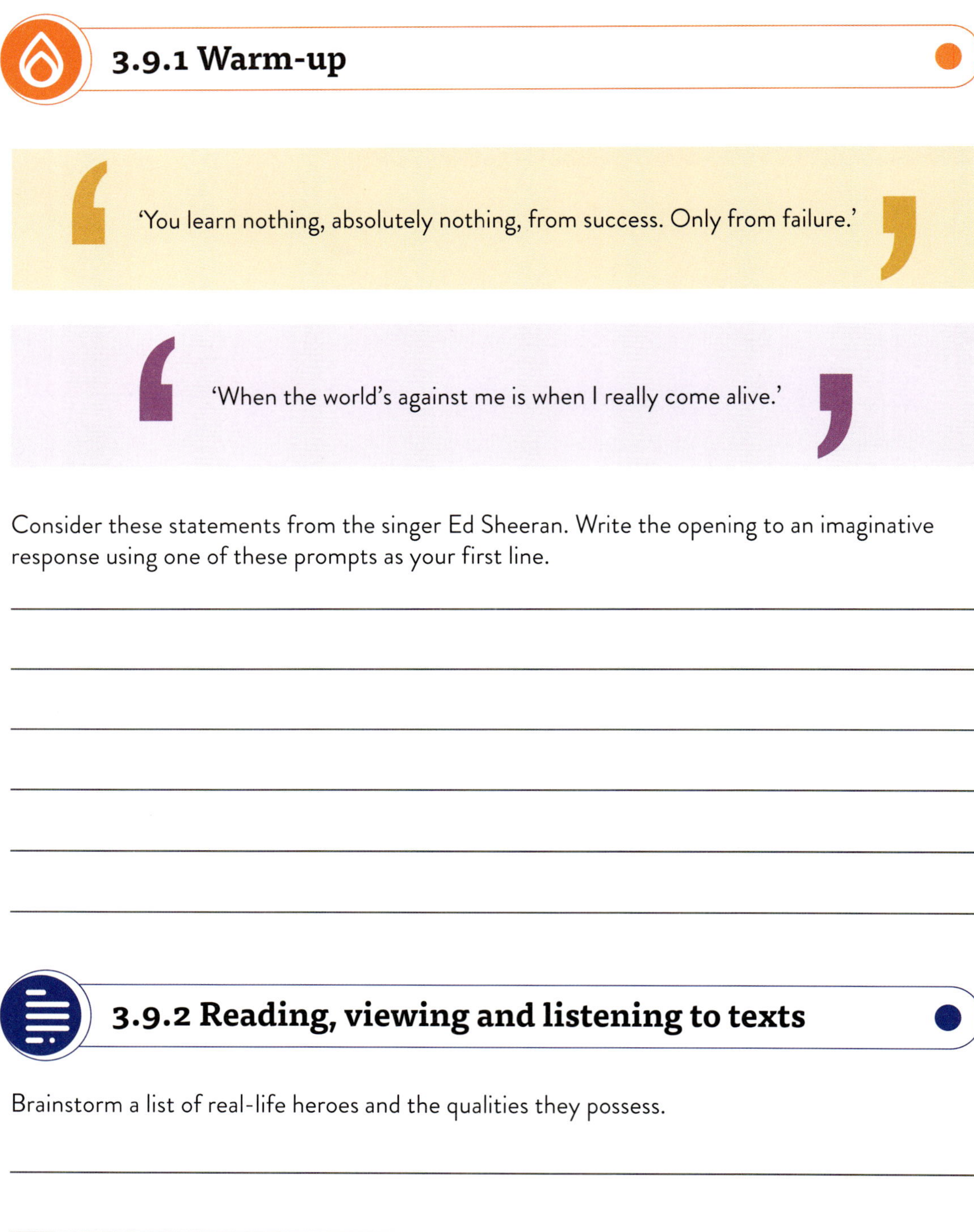

3.9.1 Warm-up

> 'You learn nothing, absolutely nothing, from success. Only from failure.'

> 'When the world's against me is when I really come alive.'

Consider these statements from the singer Ed Sheeran. Write the opening to an imaginative response using one of these prompts as your first line.

____

____

____

____

____

____

3.9.2 Reading, viewing and listening to texts

Brainstorm a list of real-life heroes and the qualities they possess.

____

____

Read the following flash fiction.

What Heroes Do

By Heather Kuehl

Christopher and Emily Kesley met the old-fashioned way. At least, that's what Kesley told me. He told me a lot when we served together. About his childhood, his family, his wife.

Dear Mrs. Kesley,

I pause, examining what I had just written. The curve of the M. The sharpness of the K. It seems wrong; not right. After all he had told me about Emily, this just felt too formal.

You don't know her, I remind myself. You two have never met.

Shaking my head, I crumple the sheet of paper and toss it toward the waste basket. It misses, landing among the other sheets of crumpled paper on the floor. Who would have thought this would be so hard.

'Honey, come to bed.'

I glance up at the doorway. My wife is leaning against the frame ...

When I don't answer, she walks over and picks up one of the balls of paper from the floor and smooths it out. Reading over the words, she gives me a sad smile.

'You'll see her tomorrow, Frank. Tell her then.'

'Tell her what? Hi, I'm Frank Glassman. I'm the reason your husband is dead. Sorry.'

'Now, you know that isn't true.'

I cradle my head in my hands. 'Go to bed, Krista. I'll be there in a minute.'

Krista sighs and places the sheet of paper on my desk. She knows better than most how I feel. Kissing the top of my head, she leaves me alone with the pen and paper. Pulling a fresh sheet out, I poise my pen to start again.

Dear

He had told me all about her. Her eyes. Her smile. How she hummed when she cooked or cleaned. How

IDENTIFY

As you read, underline the ideas about heroism.

INTERPRET

Discuss what you think 'served together' is alluding to. Is this a typical representation of a hero?

The writer is using structure in an interesting way. Kuehl switches between the present action, the letter and the past. This technique is called '**flashback**'.

IDENTIFY

UNDERLINE where the writer is using the second person pronoun 'you'. Think about the purpose of this.

PAUSE & PREDICT

Pause here and discuss with a partner what internal conflict Glassman is struggling with. How do you think the story will end?

she prided herself on her garden. He told me that she wanted nothing more than to be a mother, a blessing that she discovered soon after he was deployed. My hand shakes. His daughter was born just last month. He'd never get to see the woman his daughter would become.

The roadside bomb blew up the first part of our convoy, sending shrapnel and debris into the Hum-vee I was driving. I lost control and we hit something, sending the vehicle into a roll that left me pinned inside. Kesley fought his way over, pulling out Raines and Albright before reaching for me. I was lucky. A couple of scrapes and bruises; nothing major. He smiled, made some joke that I can't remember, as his eyes gazed over my shoulder. Grabbing my shoulders, he shoved me back and used his body to shield me from the enemy gun fire. He was dead before he hit the ground.

If I wasn't driving ...

If we hadn't crashed ...

He'd still be alive.

Why did he decide that my life was more important than his own?

I crumble the sheet and pull out a fresh page.

Shots ring out, and I clutch the envelope in my hand. I glance up at Emily as they hand her the neatly folded flag. She holds it to her chest, her eyes staring unseeingly at the ground. The priest describes how her husband was a hero, and how their country needs more men like him. Raines and Albright tell stories about him, agreeing with the priest's sentiments. Krista wraps an arm around my waist, her red rimmed eyes careful not to look at me. Before I know it, it's over. People are giving Emily their condolences, saying words that are meant to comfort. I look at the envelope in my hands. Words are never enough.

Krista hugs Emily, giving her our condolences and reminding her that she is always welcome in our home. Emily nods, dabbing at her red eyes with a tissue. My heart lurches as Krista steps away and Emily turns her bright blue eyes to me. I shake her hand, hand her the envelope, and quickly follow Krista to the car. I can't see her face when she reads the truth in my words.

I wait as Raines pulls out in front of me, tapping my fingers impatiently on the steering wheel.

'Frank.'

I look over at Krista and she points out my window. Emily is hurrying over to us, the open letter in her hands, and it was then that I can hear her calling my name. I freeze.

DISCUSS

Discuss why you think Kuehl includes these details about Kesley's wife.

DISCUSS

Discuss the effect of these short, stand-alone sentences. How do they help to convey Glassman's internal struggle?

INTERPRET

Ellipsis is a technique where the writer places '...' to show the sentences aren't finished. Consider what this indicates about Glassman's emotional state.

'Go. Talk to her.'

'I can't.'

Krista glares at me. 'You can and you will. Go.'

Sighing, I open the car door and step out. Emily slows down when she sees that I'm not going to drive away, walking the rest of the way over to me. She looks up at me, tears glittering in her eyes.

'Is this true?' she asks. He was right. Her voice is like the birds in spring. She holds the letter out to me.

'Yes.' I can't meet her eyes. How can I, when it should have been me.

I gasp as she wraps me in a hug, pressing her cheek against the ribbons on my dress uniform. I expected yelling; hitting even. But this?

'What ...?'

'You didn't do anything wrong.'

I start to stutter as I try to find the words to convey how I feel. I didn't understand it; why did Kesley decide that my life was more important than his own?

Emily grabs both of my hands up in hers. 'He did what he was put on this Earth to do, Glassman. He saved your life. It's what heroes do.'

Emily turns back toward the grave leaving me standing by the car. I climb back in the car as the sun peaks out from behind the clouds. Krista is staring at me as I drive out of the cemetery, not saying a word as we get on the interstate and head home.

INTERPRET

In the last paragraph, the reference to the sun symbolises an idea and reinforces the message of the story. Think about how the description of the sun does this.

3.9.3 Understanding and responding to texts A

1 Find an example from the flash fiction that supports the view that heroes are born, not made.

____

____

____

Read these two definitions of heroes:

'A hero is someone who has given his or her life to something bigger than oneself.' – Joseph Campbell

'A hero is an ordinary individual who finds the strength to persevere and endure in spite of overwhelming obstacles.' – Christopher Reeve

2 Explain how the flash fiction communicates the same ideas about heroism. Use examples from the text to support your ideas.

Are there any real-life heroes in our communities?

In Australia one way that we celebrate our local heroes is through the 'Australian of the Year' awards. The people who are chosen in each category are often unknown to the general public until they are awarded this accolade. They have no great super-power like a literary or film hero and they are invariably the 'unsung' heroes of our families, our communities, our state and our nation.

Search online for the Australians of the year past and present.

3.9.4 Expressing ideas and composing texts A and B

Using the following list, you are going to work with a partner on the next two tasks to explore the life and times of some local heroes. These can be completed in your workbook or electronically.

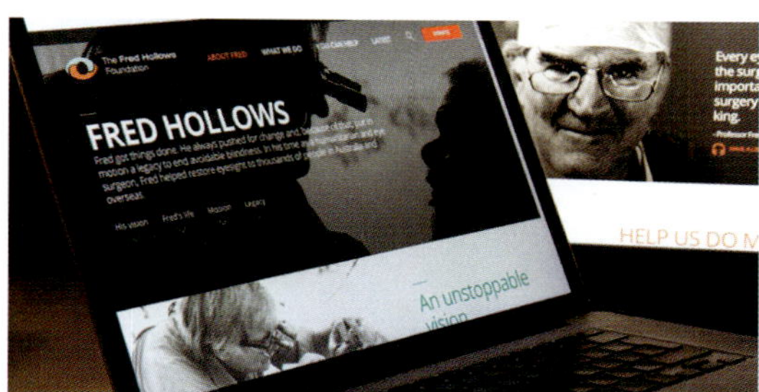

Fred Hollows – Ophthalmologist who restored sight to many Australians and many others around the world

Aunty Dr Matilda House – Ngambri-Ngunnawal Elder and advocate for Aboriginal and Torres Strait Islander rights, particularly in the areas of health and education

Cathy Freeman – Athlete, community leader and award-winning children's writer

Eddie Mabo – Torres Strait Islander community leader and land rights campaigner

Johnathan Thurston – NRL legend who works with Aboriginal and Torres Strait Islander communities to lift family wellbeing

Ian Frazer – Immunologist who co-developed the HPV vaccine, which has been instrumental in preventing cancers triggered by the HPV virus

Rosie Batty – Campaigner against domestic violence

Tim Costello – One of Australia's most respected community leaders and a sought after voice on social justice issues, leadership and ethics

You can choose the same local hero for more than one task and build on the depth of your knowledge or you can decide to choose a different hero each time to create breadth in your knowledge.

Task 1: Hero profiles

With your partner, select one local hero from the list or choose a local hero of your own. Research your hero and create a fan page for a website or blog.
Your piece should include the hero's:

- name and occupation
- background and achievements
- contributions to the community
- challenges faced
- personal qualities that make them a hero.

Extension activity

Each pair presents their hero profile to the class, sharing the reasons why they consider their chosen local hero to be worth celebrating and how they have made a positive impact on their community.

Task 2: Hero interviews

Plan a mock interview with a hero and then record the interview you have designed. Each pair should choose a hero from the previous list or one from their own research. Together, write a list of open-ended questions related to the hero's background, accomplishments and community involvement.

Facilitate the mock interviews, where one of you is the interviewer and the other the 'local hero'. You could swap around halfway through if you wish.

You should either record your interview to be watched by your peers or perform your interview in front of your class.

Students should actively listen and take notes as they listen to the interviews.

After the interviews, as a class, discuss what qualities and characteristics make someone a local hero. Reflect on the importance of recognising and celebrating local heroes.

Open-ended questions will not be answered by a yes or no response but encourage the questioned party to speak at greater length for their interviewer.

Who are your local heroes?

3.9.5 Chapter reflection

Let's return to the unit inquiry question: ***How do authors depict heroes and villains in literature and how do these representations evolve over time?***

How did reading the texts in this chapter influence your understanding of what makes a hero?

____

____

____

____

My local hero

Think about a local hero who you know. Reflect on all that you have learned about heroes in this chapter: Are heroes born or made? Are there real-life heroes in our communities? Who are your local heroes?

To demonstrate your reflections on this chapter, create a visual representation of a local hero. You can draw a portrait, create a collage or design a comic strip.

You will need blank paper, coloured pens, glue, old magazines or images from the internet.

Think about someone you know personally and consider a local hero, whether it's a family member, neighbour, teacher or someone else from your community. You might like to reflect on a particular heroic act they have done.

In this task you might like to consider:

- background information about the hero, including a heroic act and its significance to an individual or to the community
- details about the local hero involved, their motivations and the challenges they faced
- the positive impact the heroic act had on individuals or the community as a whole
- reflections on the qualities and characteristics demonstrated by local heroes.

Unit 3: **Summative assessment**

The summative assessment options below provide opportunities to demonstrate your achievement of the following outcomes and focus areas:

Outcome	EN5-RVL-01 Reading, viewing and listening to texts	EN5-URA-01 Understanding and responding to texts A	EN4-URC-01 Understanding and responding to texts C	EN5-ECA-01 Expressing ideas and composing texts A	EN5-ECB-01 Expressing ideas and composing texts B
	Reading viewing and listening for meaning	Code and convention	Literary value	Writing Text Features	Planning, monitoring and revising
				Representing	
	Reading for challenge, interest and enjoyment	Characterisation		Text features	
				Word-level language	
	Reflecting	Narrative		Speaking	

Option 1: Speech

'Well, I think there are no villains in this world. There are just misunderstood heroes.'
– Tom Hiddleston

The Sydney Writers' Festival has invited you to present a speech on the topic of villains. You are to write a speech examining why flawed characters such as villains and misunderstood heroes are so fascinating.

Explore how reading about these villains helps us to understand ourselves and make connections to others. To help illustrate and support your ideas, you are to refer to a villain studied in this unit and other examples of your own choosing. Explore how the textual examples in this unit subvert traditional conventions to shape new ideas about the villain archetype.

Be guided by the following questions to plan, write and produce your speech.

- Who are the villains that most resonated with you?
- Why are villains so attractive? Why are we drawn to characters that are supposed to repel us?
- What is the function of a villain in literature? How can you develop or challenge this idea?
- Which codes, conventions and structures can you use?
- How have you been influenced by the representation of other villains in this unit?

Option 2: Imaginative writing

'Look for the contradictions in every character, especially in your heroes and villains. No one should be what they first seem to be. Surprise the audience.' – Elia Kazan

Reimagine a hero in a contemporary setting or a different genre. Write a narrative, poem or a script in which you represent your hero in a new context. Consider what fundamental qualities of the hero you should keep and which ones you can alter and why. Your hero could be a classical hero from a Greek myth, a Shakespearean hero or another hero of your own choosing.

Be guided by the following questions to plan, write and produce your composition.

- Who is your hero?
- What is the function of your character? Does your protagonist drive action? How can you play with this (i.e. can your hero create conflict?)?
- Which codes, conventions and structures can you use to shape and create a text with new meaning?
- How have you been influenced by the representation of heroes in this unit?

Option 3: Opinion piece

'A hero is an ordinary individual who finds the strength to persevere and endure in spite of overwhelming obstacles.' – Christopher Reeve.

Time magazine is an American weekly news magazine and website published in New York City. It was founded in 1923 and has the world's largest circulation for a weekly news magazine. Time's most famous feature throughout its history has been the annual 'Person of the Year' cover story, in which *Time* recognises the individual or group of individuals who have had the biggest impact on news headlines over the past 12 months. The distinction is supposed to go to the person who, 'for good or ill', has most affected the course of the year; it is, therefore, not necessarily an honour or a reward. In the past, such figures as Adolf Hitler and Joseph Stalin have been Man of the Year.

Time magazine is running a special feature of the 'All-time 100 greatest people'. They are seeking submissions from their readers to help them compile their list. With this in mind, as well as what your learned in Chapter 9 about local heroes, you are to compose a submission to *Time* outlining the reasons your chosen hero should be included in the list of 100 greatest people. Your chosen hero can be a real person or a fictional character.*

**If you want to push yourself, choose a villain instead of a hero. It may be harder to justify why a villain should be considered 'great', but it may be an interesting challenge for you.*

Be guided by the following questions to plan, write and produce your opinion piece.

- What is the significance of your hero?
- What is your hero's legacy and enduring impact?
- How can you demonstrate what you have learned about the changing nature of the characterisation of the hero?
- What is the function of a hero in literature? How can you develop or challenge this idea?
- Which codes, conventions and structures can you use to shape and create a text with new meaning?
- How have you been influenced by the representation of heroes and villains in this unit?

Assessment as learning: self-assessment

Does my composition ...

- ☐ present a clear perspective on what makes a hero/villain?
- ☐ use appropriate structure?
- ☐ experiment with codes, conventions and structures?
- ☐ craft concise sentences?

What are two strengths of my response?

____

____

What area/s of my response do I need to refine further?

____

____

UNIT
04

A laugh a minute

Unit inquiry question:
What role does comedy play in our lives?

Humour is all around us. But do we ever stop to think about what makes something funny and why comedy is so important in our lives? In this unit, students will experience the world of comedy as they delve into the techniques behind the humour. A range of different forms of comedy such as slapstick, farce, satire and wit will be investigated. Students will be introduced to the key techniques of irony, satire, parody and word play and encouraged to consider how humour can be used to explore human nature and the follies of society.

This unit has been broken into three chapters, each with a focus on a different aspect of comedy through both literary and non-literary extracts, including digital texts.

Students will explore how comedy is a powerful communication tool with various purposes and effects. Comedy can help us to connect with each other, celebrate our creativity, challenge our perspectives, and offer a poignant critique of individuals and society.

Chapter 10

Comic beginnings

In this chapter, students will learn about the inception of the comedy genre and how it has evolved and expanded over time. Students will also explore the codes, conventions and forms of comedy.

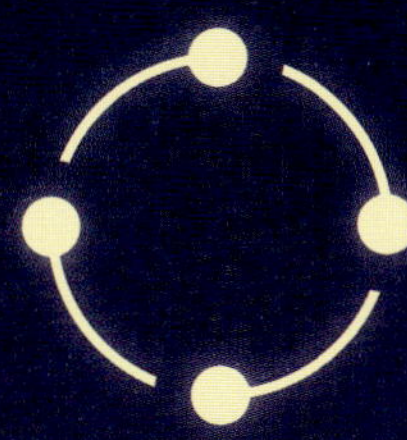

Chapter 11

Clowning around

In this chapter, students will explore the use of physical and visual comedy and understand how it is an important comic tool.

Chapter 12

Comedy is a serious business

In this final chapter, students will explore the role that comedy plays in culture, particularly in subverting or challenging socio-political situations.

The learning activities within each chapter and the summative assessment options (on page 181) provide opportunities to assess student achievement of the following outcomes:

Outcome and Focus Area	Content point
EN5-RVL-01 Reading, viewing and listening to texts	**Reading, viewing and listening for meaning**
	Investigate how layers of meaning are constructed in texts and how this shapes a reader's understanding and engagement Clarify and justify personal responses to texts, explaining how aspects of the text, such as character, genre, tone, salience or voice, position a reader and influence these personal responses
EN5-URA-01 Understanding and responding to texts A	**Code and convention**
	Analyse how language forms, features and structures, specific or conventional to a text's medium, context, purpose and audience, shape meaning, and experiment with this understanding through written, spoken, visual and multimodal responses
EN5-URB-01 Understanding and responding to texts B	**Perspective and context**
	Evaluate how texts can position audiences to accept, challenge or reject particular perspectives of the world, and reflect on this in own texts
EN5-URC-01 Understanding and responding to texts C	**Genre**
	Reflect on the evolution, adaptation, subversion and hybridity of genre in different time periods and cultural contexts, and how they demonstrate changing values
EN5-ECA-01 Expressing ideas and composing texts A	**Representing**
	Compose visual and multimodal texts to express complex ideas, using a range of digital technologies where appropriate
	Speaking
	Deliver spoken, signed or communicated texts with engaging use of intonation, emphasis, volume, pace and timing
	Word-level language
	Select technical vocabulary to write with accuracy in a range of modes and registers appropriate to audience, purpose, form and context Make vocabulary choices that enhance stylistic features of writing, and shape meaning through connotation

Chapter overview

In this chapter, you will consider what comedy is and the various forms it can take. You will learn about how comedy began and how it has evolved and expanded over time. Through this, you will learn about the typical conventions, forms and features of comedy. This will help you to begin to examine the purpose of comedy: is it merely to make fun of people or does humour play a more important role?

Success criteria: In this chapter, I will be successful when I can ...

- read, view and understand extracts from prose, plays, films and TV shows
- understand and identify different types of comedy and comedic conventions
- analyse how comedic codes and conventions create humour
- experiment with using comedic codes and conventions to create humour in my own compositions
- reflect on the evolution of the comic genre in different time periods and cultural contexts and how they show changing values.

Chapter inquiry questions

- What is comedy?
- How did comedy begin?
- How has comedy changed?
- What are the codes and conventions of comedy?

Key vocabulary

- Subjective
- Satire
- Incongruity
- Farce
- Dramatic irony

What is comedy?

Comedy is an expansive genre, and it exists in every place and time, and has always been extremely popular. If you were to define this genre, what would you say? Your definition of comedy is influenced by your life experiences and personal taste. Some people define comedy as anything that causes us to be amused and to laugh. Others see that comedy is the act of telling jokes, while others believe that comedy is about making us feel uncomfortable and unsettled. Many people see that comedy is designed to give us an escape from daily life or difficult situations.

Even if you don't find these texts funny, does that mean they're not comedy? What makes us laugh is **subjective** and we can't always agree on what is funny. But perhaps what we can agree on is the tools composers use to create comedy.

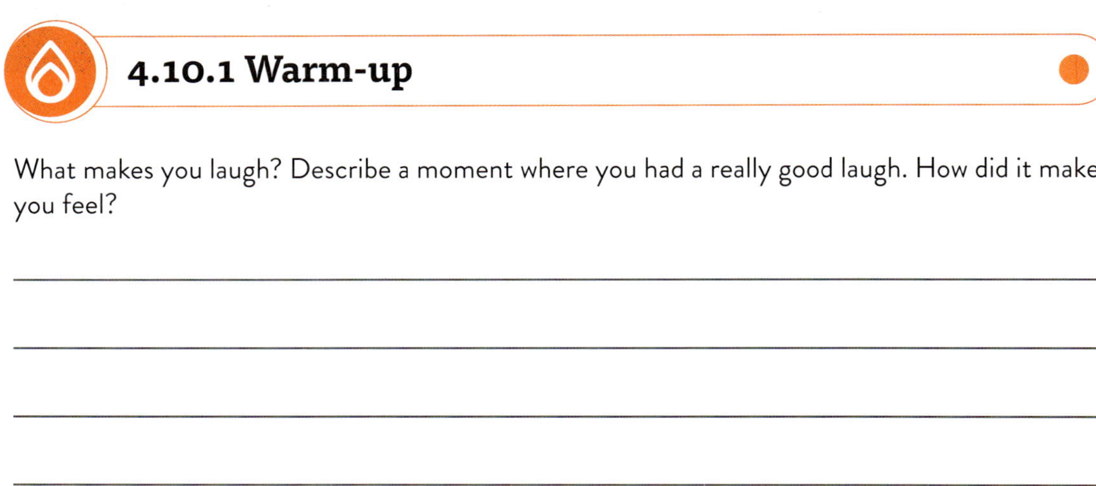

4.10.1 Warm-up

What makes you laugh? Describe a moment where you had a really good laugh. How did it make you feel?

Essentially, the foundation of comedy relies on the unexpected. We are often lead down one path, being set up to expect one thing, only to be completely surprised by an unexpected occurrence. This is the premise of most jokes. You will learn in this chapter how flouting expectations is the backbone of comedy.

VOCABULARY

Subjective
adjective: something that is related to or characteristic of an individual; personal.

4.10.2 Reading, viewing and listening to texts

Look at this cartoon from the magazine Punch.

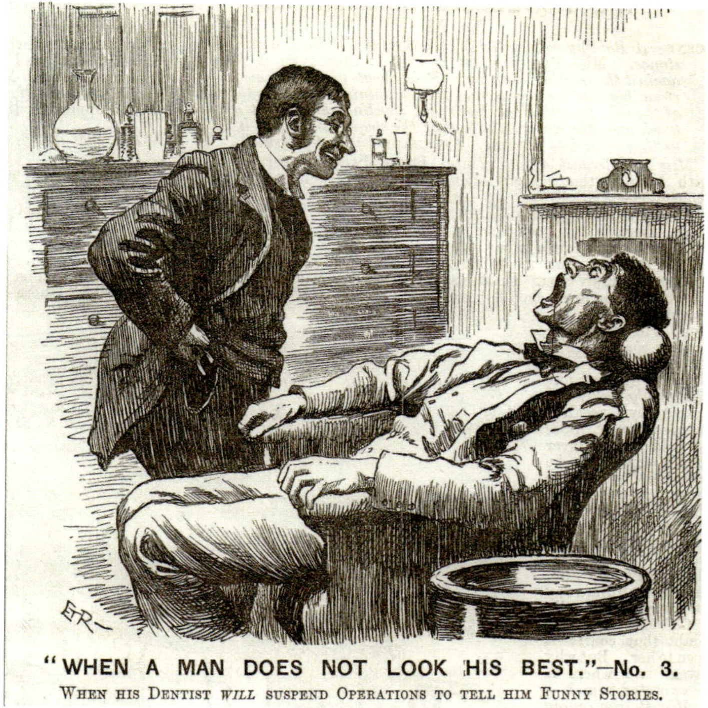

"WHEN A MAN DOES NOT LOOK HIS BEST."—No. 3.
WHEN HIS DENTIST *WILL* SUSPEND OPERATIONS TO TELL HIM FUNNY STORIES.

VOCABULARY

Incongruity
adjective: not consistent or compatible with something else, or what you would expect.

This Victorian cartoon, created in 1891, is capturing a very common circumstance where a patient waits with his mouth wide open, a very compromising situation, as his dentist tells him jokes. Now, when you look at this cartoon, you may not laugh, you may not even giggle. But you can appreciate what the cartoon is doing to be funny. The cartoon is using two main comic features to create comedy: exaggeration (the body language of both men) and **incongruity** (we do not expect the dentist to turn into a comedian, it feels out of place).

1 Explain why exaggeration or incongruity make us laugh.

____

____

____

Read the following extracts, then respond to the questions below.

My Life is a Wedgie

By Gretel Killeen

Anyway, Miss Priss, who is desperate to prove that I'm dead, has replied that dead people always twitch. And Bum Face is saying that the best way to see if I really am dead is to place a packet of chocolate biscuits in the corner of the room and leave me with them while they go watch the telly. The idea is that if I'm alive I won't be able to resist the biscuits and then in the morning they'll have all disappeared ... thus proving the fact that I'm not dead. This is exactly the test my family did on my Grandpa in 1992. But in the morning, much to everyone's shock, both he and the chocolate biscuits had gone. (In fact, he wasn't found until three years later in Woolgoolga. And he was still wearing the same pyjamas, carrying the very same unopened packet of biscuits and working part-time as a garden gnome.)

(Page 14)

Sometimes I wonder what it must be like to be able to walk down the street with pride, but I guess I actually won't really know what that feels like until the divorce from my family comes through. Ever since the first minute I was born and saw my googly-faced know-nothing parents I've been trying to prove I'm not related to my family. In fact my friend Mona says I should go the whole way and suggest that I don't even know them. Of course there is photographic evidence that would suggest I do know my family, because we're together in a thousand shots. But the main thing is I'm not smiling in any of them so my argument is that I was kidnapped.

(Page 16)

Lying on the floor pretending to be dead is actually not as interesting as I'd hope (but then again, nothing in my life is). I wish Prince William would kidnap me. I think I'd make a perfect princess. Of course I could never let Mum know I was getting married because she'd insist that I wear her old wedding frock and veil, which are both made entirely from bubble wrap. Not that there's anything wrong with bubble wrap. I mean, it's certainly more interesting than my sisters, but it's really noisy to sit down in.

(Page 17)

2 Write down your first impressions.

____

____

3 In pairs, discuss what could be considered amusing about these extracts. Then, fill in the table.

What was amusing	What was not amusing

4 Share your responses with the class.

5 These extracts from *My Life is a Wedgie* also uses exaggeration. Find an example of exaggeration and explain how this creates humour.

JOKE OF THE DAY!

I said to the Gym instructor 'Can you teach me to do the splits?' He said, 'How flexible are you?' I said, 'I can't make Tuesdays.'

How did comedy begin?

The origins

As you've started to explore some comic texts, have you noticed how some things about comedy haven't changed? Perhaps there are some things that we will always find funny.

The earliest known examples of comedy come from Ancient Greece, over two thousand years ago. Greek playwrights created stories with amusing characters who triumphed over difficult circumstances, producing lots of hilarity along the way. They used **satire** and **farce**, as well as classic comedic codes and conventions, such as mistaken identity, crude jokes, disguises and insults. These stories are often light-hearted, celebrating how laughter can triumph over adversity, and they always end happily. Sound familiar?

The word 'comedy' comes from Greek: *komos*, 'songs of merrimakers'. Originally, comedy referred to a genre of drama during the Dionysia festivals of ancient Athens. These comedies were loud and boisterous drunken affairs. Later, in Medieval and Renaissance times, comedy changed to a play or poem in which the main characters thwart disaster and have a happy ending. These stories didn't have to be funny. Sometimes, in fact, they were serious. Interestingly, it wasn't until the nineteenth and twentieth centuries that comedy came to be associated with humour.

VOCABULARY

Satire
noun: expose and criticise flaws and weaknesses through humour, irony, exaggeration and ridicule.

Farce
noun: a type of comedy that creates complicated, exaggerated, absurd and ridiculous situations. You will see a lot of physical comedy, nonsense, parody and satire in farce.

Shakespearean comedy

In Shakespeare's time, 'comedy' had a very different meaning to today. A Shakespearean comedy didn't have to be funny, but there are certainly very humorous moments in many of Shakespeare's plays. Typically, these comedies have happy endings, usually finishing with weddings, and the situation is emphasised more than the characters. Shakespeare's comedies are famous for their **dramatic irony**, situational humour, slapstick, disguise and word play.

VOCABULARY

Dramatic irony
noun: a situation where the audience knows more than the characters; comments and actions made by the characters take on extra or unusual meanings.

Extension activity

Scan the QR code or research online and read the article 'An introduction to Shakespeare's comedy' by John Mullan.

Outline the main characteristics of Shakespeare's comedies.

____

____

____

____

____

4.10.3 Reading, viewing and listening to texts

Let's look at a classic example of one of Shakespeare's comedies, *A Midsummer Night's Dream*. We are going to look at a scene that exhibits Shakespeare's fantastic use of physical, visual and verbal comedy.

The following extract is from Act 3, Scene 1. In this scene, a group of actors meet to rehearse a play and Puck, the prankster fairy, decides to have some fun. He places a donkey's head on one of the actors, Bottom. So, when Bottom re-enters the stage, his fellow actors are completely surprised and terrified, but Bottom is unaware and continues rehearsing his lines.

A Midsummer Night's Dream

By William Shakespeare

[Enter Puck, and Bottom with an ass's head]

BOTTOM
'If I were fair, Thisbe, I were only thine.'

QUINCE
O monstrous! O strange! We are haunted.
Pray, masters, fly, masters! Help!
[Quince, Snug, Flute, Snout and Starveling exit]

PUCK
I'll follow you, I'll lead you about a round,
Through bog, through bush, through brake, through brier
...
[Exit]

BOTTOM
Why do they run away? This is a knavery of them to make me afeard.
[Enter Snout]

SNOUT
O Bottom, thou art chang'd! What do I see on thee?

BOTTOM
What do you see? You see an ass-head of your own, do you?
[Exit Snout]
[Enter Quince]

QUINCE
Bless thee. Bottom, bless thee! Thou art translated.

DISCUSS

One comic technique Shakespeare uses is characterisation. Bottom is a comic character who becomes the butt (pun intended) of many jokes. He is a self-important know-it-all, so we laugh at his expense, enjoying the fact that he has been brought down.

Discuss how does Shakespeare creates visual humour in this moment.

Shakespeare uses dramatic irony to create humour. Bottom is unaware that he has a donkey head.

Each time Bottom says 'nay'-sounding words imagine the actor 'neighing' (e.g. when he says 'knavery', it would sound like 'neigh-very').

To intensify the joke, Shakespeare creates verbal humour through puns (puns are words with similar or identical sounds, but with different meanings).

When Bottom thinks his fellow actors are playing a trick on him, he says that they are making 'an ass' of him (ass is another word for donkey), and we laugh at his unintended double meaning.

[Exit]

BOTTOM
I see their knavery. This is to make an ass of me, to fright me, if they could; but I will not stir from this place, do what they can. I will walk up and down here, and I will sing, that they shall hear I am not afraid.
[Sings]

TITANIA [Awaking]
What angel wakes me from my flow'ry bed?

BOTTOM [Sings]
The finch, the sparrow, and the lark,
The plainsong cuckoo grey,
Whose note full many a man doth mark,
And dares not answer nay –

For indeed, who would set his wit to so foolish a bird? Who would give a bird the lie, though he cry 'cuckoo' never so?

TITANIA
I pray thee, gentle mortal, sing again.
Mine ear is much enamored of thy note;
So is mine eye enthralled to thy shape;
And thy fair virtue's force (perforce) doth move me
On the first view to say, to swear, I love thee.

BOTTOM
Methinks, mistress, you should have little reason for that. And yet, to say the truth, reason and love keep little company together now-a-days. The more the pity that some honest neighbors will not make them friends. Nay, I can **gleek** upon occasion.

TITANIA
Thou art as wise as thou art beautiful.

Earlier in the scene, Puck plays a prank on Titania by dropping a love potion in her eyes while she sleeps. Whoever (or whatever) Titania sees first upon opening her eyes, she will fall desperately, madly in love with.

Things become farcical when Titania awakes and falls in love with Bottom.

Circle the line that reveals the moment when Titania falls in love with Bottom.

VOCABULARY

Gleek
verb: make a joke

1 Dramatic irony is created when Bottom is not aware that he has a donkey's head, but the other characters are (as well as the audience). Identify and write down three examples of dramatic or verbal irony in his lines.

2 Titania dotes on Bottom. Identify two examples of verbal irony in Titania's words/phrases. Write them down.

3 Explain how the humour of Titania loving Bottom is enhanced due to Titania being the Queen of the Fairies.

4.10.4 Understanding and responding to texts A and B

1 Another visual comic element that Shakespeare creates is sudden appearances and disappearances through the characters' entrances and exits. Highlight the characters' entrances and exits and explain how these create humour.

2 Write a paragraph analysing how this scene fits in the comedy genre. Identify and analyse two comic features. In your response, consider how Shakespeare uses Bottom to create physical, visual and verbal comedy. Specifically, this is done through comic features, like exaggeration, incongruity, farce and irony.

Extension activity

1 Watch the following performance. This is from earlier in Act 3, Scene 1.

Scan the QR code to view the performance.

2 How has the director added and used technology to create more humour in this scene?

3 In your opinion, do we need to add contemporary references to make Shakespeare funny?

4.10.5 Expressing ideas and composing texts A

1 Show your understanding of the comedy in this scene by creating a visual representation. Find or create an image of a humorous moment in this scene and write a caption from the script underneath to highlight the humour.

2 Making fun of people being in love is one of Shakespeare's favourite jokes. Write about two characters falling in love but put a humorous twist on it to make fun of how people behave when they fall in love. Use comic tools like exaggeration, subversion and irony.

Extension activity

In your English notebook, write a farce scene that involves miscommunication, mistakes and dramatic irony. Your scene needs to start with the line, 'I wouldn't go that way if I were you,' and end with, 'I told you we wouldn't get out of this alive'.

How has comedy changed?

While there are some things that we will always find funny, the comedy genre continues to expand and evolve over time. In the nineteenth century, clowns, mimes and musical theatre were the popular form of comedy. With the invention of silent film in the twentieth century, the genre changed direction, seeing the popularity of famous comic actors like Charlie Chaplin and Buster Keaton. Things continued to evolve once sound films, and then TV, came into being and stand-up comedy, talk and skit shows started to entertain audiences. In the 1960s the social and political climate changed. Comedy reflected this change and began to address these issues. With the invention of YouTube in 2005, 'at-home' comedians could produce their own comic texts.

JOKE OF THE DAY!

A woman gets on a bus with her baby. The bus driver says: 'Ugh, that's the ugliest baby I've ever seen!' The woman walks to the rear of the bus and sits down, fuming. She says to a man next to her: 'The driver just insulted me!' The man says: 'You go up there and tell him off. Go on, I'll hold your monkey for you.'

4.10.6 Reading, viewing and listening to texts

1 In groups or individually, look up these comic texts and watch a short scene. As you view these, fill in the table to record your impressions.

	What could be considered amusing in this clip?
The Keystone Kops (1910)	
Abbott and Costello (1938)	
I Love Lucy (1956)	
Fawlty Towers (1975)	
The Simpsons (1995)	
Seinfeld (1995)	
The Office (2009)	
Bo Burnham (2022)	

2 What two changes in the comedy genre did you notice?

3 What similarities did you notice in these clips?

4 Which clips did you find the most amusing? Why?

5 Compare your responses with a partner's. Did you find the same clips amusing?

What are the codes and conventions of comedy?

As we have seen, what makes us laugh is subjective, which means that comedy is a broad and multi-dimensional genre. Comedy appears in lots of different shapes and sizes. Some of the different types of comedy are physical comedy, verbal comedy, situational comedy, romantic comedy, dark comedy, parody, satire and farce.

4.10.7 Reading, viewing and listening to texts

1 Read the information on the types of comedy in the table. In the last column some examples have been included. From your own reading and viewing, add some more examples.

Types of comedy

Type	Meaning	Example
Physical comedy or slapstick	Exaggerated body movements, violence, clowning, physical gags, ridiculous situations	Charlie Chaplin, Mr Bean
Verbal comedy	Witty wordplay, sarcasm, irony, puns, double entendre	
Situational comedy	Characters find themselves in awkward, amusing situations, humour comes from how the characters react	Seinfeld
Romantic comedy	Romantic relationships that are thwarted, resulting in situational comedy, but there is a happy ending	
Dark comedy	Light-hearted treatment of serious subjects	

Spoof or parody	Uses imitation to ridicule another text	Scary Movie
Satire	Mocks flaws and weaknesses of society or politics	
Farce	Extreme exaggeration of characters and improbable situations caused by miscommunication or mistaken identity	Home Alone

2 Within these types of comedy there are also identifiable comedic codes and conventions, common elements that are used in all types that clearly make them comedy. Watch the comic texts again and identify the comedic conventions used.

	What comedic conventions are used?
The Keystone Kops (1910)	
Abbott and Costello (1938)	
I Love Lucy (1956)	
Fawlty Towers (1975)	
The Simpsons (1995)	
Seinfeld (1995)	
The Office (2009)	
Bo Burnham (2022)	

3 Which clips used more than one type of comedy? Did this make the texts more humorous?

___

___

___

4 Did you notice any common conventions that were used in more than one text?

5 What personal favourites would you add to the list?

4.10.8 Chapter reflection

Comedy has been an important part of society for centuries because it allows people to laugh at themselves. Throughout this chapter, you have learned about the beginning of comedy and how it has changed over time.

1 I enjoy this type of comedy: ______ because ...

2 In this chapter, the activity that I liked the most was ______ because ...

3 What is comedy? Create a mind-map outlining what you have learned about comedy so far. Include ideas about how you would define the genre.

4 How has comedy changed? The texts we have looked at in this chapter show that the comedy genre has changed. These changes occur due to a society's shift in attitudes and values.

a What has stood out to you as the biggest changes in the comedy genre?

b What have you noticed are the things that haven't changed? Why do you think that is the case?

5 Choose one text from the chapter. What does this text show about the society and time it was created?

6 Let's consider the unit inquiry question: ***What role does comedy play in our lives?*** Explain what you think the role of comedy is. Refer to at least one text studied in this chapter and another of your own choosing.

CHAPTER 11

CLOWNING AROUND

Chapter overview

In this chapter, you will learn about the power of physical comedy. Physical comedy, one of the oldest types, is universal and inclusive and is the foundation of many humorous films, comics, cartoons and advertising.

You will dive into one of the main types of physical comedy, slapstick. Part of the appeal of slapstick is that you don't need advanced linguistic skills to understand the jokes of the banana peel or the flying pie. But you will come to realise that great slapstick requires advance skills in comedic writing.

Finally, this chapter will explore why we laugh at comedic characters and consider what comic tools they use to make us laugh. You might start to appreciate that physical comedy is timeless and that it plays an important role in our lives.

Success criteria: In this chapter, I will be successful when I can ...

- read, view and understand extracts from visual and print texts
- understand and identify different comedic conventions used in physical comedy and slapstick
- analyse how physical comedy conventions create humour
- experiment with using physical comedy to create humour in my own compositions
- reflect on the timeless nature of physical comedy.

Chapter inquiry questions

- What is physical comedy?
- What can we learn from slapstick comedy?
- Why do we laugh at comedic characters?

Key vocabulary

- Slapstick
- Exaggeration
- Inversion
- Anticipation

What is physical comedy?

For thousands of years physical comedy has been a big part of the genre of comedy. As you will see in the following activities, the humour of physical comedy comes from bodily movements and exaggerated actions. Physical comedy can include slapstick, clowning, mime, physical stunts or making funny faces. Most importantly, the jokes in physical comedy are delivered visually, no dialogue is needed, and it's all about great staging designed to get the laughs.

4.11.1 Warm-up

As a class, discuss an opening to an imaginative text using the following as your starting sentence:

'Are you sure you want to do that? The last time you tried, it exploded.'

4.11.2 Reading, viewing and listening to texts

Look at this classic comic book cover from 1947.

1 What aspects of physical and visual comedy is it using?

____

____

2 What do you think will happen next?

____

____

____

3 Look at these advertisements. For each one, identify what comedic conventions are used to create humour.

What can we learn from slapstick comedy?

Slapstick is a type of physical comedy that has been a popular comedic style for centuries. Its humour is based on tripping, slapping, **pratfalls**, practical jokes, mistakes, ridiculous situations, extensive chasing and props. In slapstick, the exaggerated violence is harmless and light-hearted; no one actually gets hurt.

THE HISTORY OF THE 'SLAPSTICK'

The term 'slapstick' comes from a prop used in the physical comedy of the *commedia dell'arte*, a sixteenth century style of Italian theatre. The 'slap stick' was made of two thin slats of wood. When an actor was pretending to hit another actor, it made a loud 'slap' sound, which made it look and sound worse than it really was.

VOCABULARY

Pratfall
noun: when someone falls over and lands on their behind, often seen as comical or embarrassing.

4.11.3 Reading, viewing and listening to texts

1 Search online and watch the classic Three Stooges 'Pie Fight' scene.

a Would the sketch have been as funny if you'd read it rather than watched it? Explain why or why not.

b What slapstick techniques are used in this scene?

2 In pairs, conduct some research into the history of slapstick, finding out who are the top five slapstick comedians from 1915 to today.

a Using the information that you have found, create a timeline, adding each year and comedian to the timeline below.

1915 — today

b Looking at your timeline, what slapstick trends do you notice?

c Does it seem to be more popular at a particular time? Why do you think that might be?

d Add some more modern-day comic actors who use physical comedy.

3 Can you think of modern examples, films or TV shows, that use slapstick? Discuss with a partner.

4.11.4 Reading, viewing and listening to texts

Slapstick is more than just throwing a pie, slapping and falling over. There are key structural devices that are used to develop the humour. These are: **inversion**, repetition, anticipation, escalation and timing.

VOCABULARY

Inversion
noun: anything that is reversed in position, changed to the contrary or turned upside down.

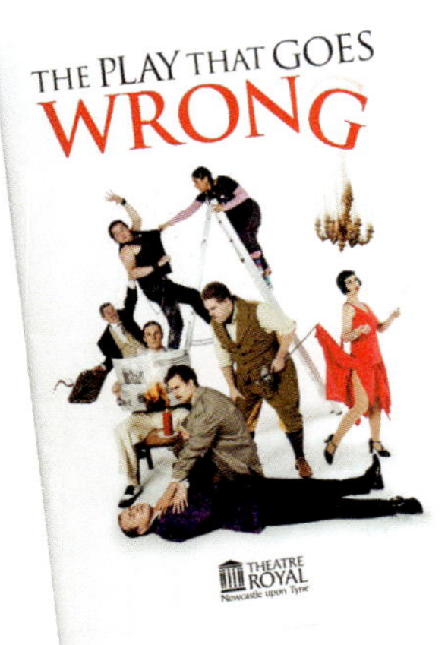

Let's read an extract from the play *The One-Act Play that Goes Wrong* by Henry Lewis, Jonathan Sayer and Henry Shields. In the play, the inept and accident-prone Cornley Polytechnic Drama Society attempt to perform a 1920s murder mystery. As you can imagine, there is much that goes wrong, and so much hilarity comes from their mistakes and attempts to keep the play going – the show must go on! An added layer of humour is created with this common 'play within a play' comic device.

Read the following extract. As you read, see if you can identify the moments where the structural devices (inversion, repetition, anticipation, escalation and timing) are used.

The One-Act Play that Goes Wrong

By Henry Lewis, Jonathan Sayer and Henry Shields

CHRIS is the head of the drama society, directed the play and plays Inspector Carter.

SANDRA plays Florence Colleymoore (fiancée of Charles, the murder victim).

ROBERT plays Thomas Colleymoore.

MAX plays Cecil Haversham (brother of Charles).

CHRIS. It's my job to ask difficult questions Miss Colleymoore, I'm sorry if this upsets you.

SANDRA. Upsets me? How dare you! My fiancé was murdered in this very room, a matter of hours ago! I find your manner most unbefitting! I shall make a formal complaint to Scotland Yard.

CHRIS. Scotland Yard will not listen to the complaints of a murderess!

SANDRA. You diabolical beast! How can you? I won't stand for this, Inspector! Accuse me again and you'll be sor ...

IDENTIFY

Identify the things that go wrong.

PAUSE AND DISCUSS

By this stage of the play, the audience has already witnessed many things going wrong. The audience will be **anticipating** more mistakes and problems for the actors. Discuss what you anticipate will go wrong in the scene.

Robert bursts in, followed by Max; the door hits Sandra sharply on the head and she collapses, unconscious.

ROBERT. What's all this shouting!

MAX. What is this, Inspector?

All register that Sandra is on the floor.

CHRIS. I'm merely interviewing Miss Colleymoore, nothing more.

MAX. Florence, calm down, stop shouting!

Sandra remains unconscious.

ROBERT. She's having one of her episodes. Snap out of it, you're hysterical!

Sandra remains unconscious.

MAX. Florence! Where are you going?

Sandra remains unconscious.

ROBERT. Come back here this instant!

Sandra remains unconscious.

She's run off. I'll fetch her back. You stay here Cecil, I daresay the Inspector has some questions for you; you were Charles' brother after all.

Robert exits.

Robert, Jonathan and Annie peer through the curtain together to see if Sandra is alright.

MAX. And didn't I know it, Charles patronised and embarrassed me throughout our childhood. He always thought he knew best, and Father always took his side. If he ever didn't get his way, he was unbearable.

Now Annie, Robert and Jonathan all reach through the window and start to lift Sandra out under the curtains.

CHRIS. He sounds far from the ideal brother. It sounds like you hated one another.

MAX. I won't lie Inspector, Charles and I never truly saw eye to eye, but if you're suggesting I had something to do with his death, you're mistaken.

CHRIS. I see. It's a dark night, Cecil.

Chris pulls the curtains open, revealing Robert, Annie and Jonathan. They all freeze and try not to be seen. Sandra is held unconscious, in an awkward position.

INVERSION

Things are turned upside down in this play. The script represents ideas of the seriousness of murder, but what we see is the reverse. Identify an example of inversion.

DISCUSS

Stage directions convey how the non-spoken parts of the script that gives information to the actors. Discuss how important the stage directions are in this moment for creating comedy. What is the effect of the stage directions repeating 'Sandra remains unconscious'?

IDENTIFY

Underline the words in the script that directly contradict the real action on stage.

THINK

What the actors are doing in the scene is breaking the 'magic' of the theatre where the audience is supposed to suspend their disbelief. Think about how Sandra's unconscious body and the attempts to remove it off stage **subverts** expectations.

IDENTIFY

Identify examples of **exaggeration**.

ESCALATION

Here, we see a series of exaggerated acts, which **escalates** the action. Circle these moments.

MAX. Inspector?

CHRIS. You can barely even make out the trees.

MAX. What are you saying, Inspector?

CHRIS. I'm saying, Cecil, that tonight would be the perfect night for you to murder your brother.

Chris and Max turn back downstage. Robert, Annie and Jonathan continue to remove Sandra.

MAX. Inspector, please, me and my brother had our differences, but deep down we cared for one another...

CHRIS. (Offhand.) And yet you had an affair with his fiancée?

Robert, Annie and Jonathan drop Sandra and start again.

MAX. ... What on earth gave you that idea?

CHRIS. The letter I found in Charles' pocket from Miss Colleymoore to yourself ...

... Robert, Annie and Jonathan have managed to get Sandra out of the window. Annie pulls the curtains shut.

MAX. Well ... Bravo Inspector! Very good. You've found out about Florence and I, but it proves nothing. We didn't have a thing to do with Charles' murder, but I can tell you who does.

DISCUSS

At the end of the scene, the actors finally get Sandra off stage. Discuss whether this is an example of inversion, repetition, anticipation or timing.

DISCUSS

The irony in Chris's line here and the situation of the actors standing outside the window is an example of irony. Discuss how this creates comedy.

IDENTIFY

Underline the words in Max's last lines that could **suggest** he's talking to the actors after they get Sandra out the window.

1 What do you think is the most amusing part of these scenes? Explain why.

____

____

____

2 What do you think will happen at the end of the play?

____

____

3 In groups, perform this extract. Reflect on other comedic aspects you notice as you perform it.

If you would like to read the full version of this play, search for it online.

4.11.5 Understanding and responding to texts A and B

As we have seen, the play uses inversion to create slapstick comedy. Things have been reversed and turned upside down, and the audience's expectations have been flipped.

1 Explain how we expect each of the actors/characters to behave and outline how the writer has created them to behave to the contrary. Use a quotation from the play to support your answer.

2 Explain how the inversion creates slapstick comedy.

3 Throughout the play, the writer uses exaggerated violence to create humour. These scenes are represented to be humorous, causing us to laugh at the characters rather than empathise with them. Explain how these moments of exaggerated violence are humorous rather than disturbing.

4 This story introduces us to a familiar comedic situation. Can you think of other texts that use this same situation and use slapstick to create humour?

Extension activity

Shakespeare uses the 'play within a play' comic device, where his actors are also inept and things go wrong. Search online for and view Act 4, Scene 2 of *A Midsummer Night's Dream*.

1 How does this scene also use inversion and situational irony?

____

____

____

____

2 What similarities are there between Shakespeare's play within a play and *The One-Act Play that Goes Wrong*?

____

____

____

____

3 Write your own play within a play scene. Use inversion, repetition, anticipation, escalation and timing to create slapstick comedy in your scene.

____

____

____

____

____

____

____

____

____

____

Why do we laugh at comedic characters?

The comedic character has been around for hundreds of years. Charlie Chaplin is one of the most famous physical comedians of all time, using physicality to embody a comedic character. Other famous physical comedians in more recent times include: Rowan Atkinson (Mr Bean), Jim Carey, Melissa McCarthy, Will Ferrell, Frank Woodley, Amy Schumer, Jackie Chan, Sacha Baron Cohen and, of course, the Minions.

In plays, cartoons, films and TV shows, the comedic character was often created to contrast with the main characters. The comedic character can often represent the underdog, the scoundrel, the rebel or the innocent child. Sometimes, they represent all of these in one. They are incapable of following the rules and behaving correctly.

We laugh because the character is the joke. But we also laugh because they present a truth with which we identify.

4.11.6 Expressing ideas and composing texts A

The comedic actor

In pairs, create a presentation about a comedic actor. Choose an actor from the list below and research their life and legacy.

• Jim Carrey • Will Ferrell • Tina Fey • Kitty Flanagan • Ricky Gervais	• Kevin Hart • Amy Schumer • Mindy Kaling • Rebel Wilson • Ali Wong

Research the actor's:

- background information
- performances
- type of comedy and comic devices they use
- contribution to the comedy genre.

What can go wrong when ... ?

A slapstick scene can involve a comedic actor wrestling with simple everyday situations and things inevitably go wrong. The comedic actor finds themselves in ludicrous situations because of many accidents and errors.

Rowan Atkinson's Mr Bean is an excellent example of this. There's a great scene where Mr Bean is at a restaurant and unwittingly orders steak tartare (raw steak). He is revolted by the taste of it, so, instead of telling the waiter and re-ordering a meal, he goes about trying to find (creative) ways to hide bits of the steak. Much of the humour comes from the various ways Mr Bean tries to hide the steak tartare at his table (in a vase, in the sugar bowl, etc.).

For more examples, check out the following clips: 'Job Switching' from *I Love Lucy* or Laurel and Hardy's 'Playing Pool Brats'.

1 Write a scene in which you explore what can go wrong when your comedic character tries to do something simple, encounters a problem and resolves it in the most ineffective or unusual way. Choose one of the following everyday activities:

- Texting while walking down the street.
- Waiting for the bus.
- Taking your dog for a walk.
- Making some eggs on toast.

Then, work out what could go wrong and what crazy or unusual solution your comedic actor invents. Use the key structural devices of inversion, repetition, anticipation, escalation and timing.

2 Explain how you used physical comedy to create humour.

4.11.7 Chapter reflection

1 I enjoy/do not enjoy (circle one) physical comedy because ...

2 In this chapter, the activity that I liked the most was ______________ because ...

3 What is physical comedy? Create a mind-map outlining what you have learned about physical comedy.

4 Has physical comedy changed? Do we still find it funny today? Explain why/why not. Choose one text from this chapter. What does this text show about the outdated or timeless nature of physical comedy?

5 Let's return to the unit inquiry question: ***What role does comedy play in our lives?*** Based on what you have learned in this chapter, do you think physical comedy serves an important role in our lives?

Chapter 12
Laughter is a Serious Business

Chapter overview

In this chapter, you will learn that comedy does more than make us laugh. Kenneth Alford, from The School of Life, comments, 'we're used to thinking that the purpose of comedy is just to help us relax and "have a good laugh". But in fact, the mission of comedy is far grander and more world changing. We should wake up to the full potential of comedy.'

Comedy is not merely light-hearted amusement, it is a powerful tool that can provoke deep thinking. When we find something funny, it is often because it holds a kernel of truth that resonates with us. You will learn that the comedy genre serves as a vehicle to expose truths, challenge boundaries and express vital ideas. Satire is commonly employed in this genre to achieve these ends. By engaging with comic texts, we gain fresh insights into the complexities of human nature that would otherwise remain elusive.

Success criteria: In this chapter, I will be successful when I can ...

- read, view and understand extracts from visual and print texts
- understand and identify the codes and conventions of satire and when best to employ them
- analyse how satire creates humour and makes us think

Chapter inquiry questions

- What is satire?
- What are the common codes and conventions of satire?
- How can satire expose flaws and challenge ideas?
- How can I use satire to make changes in society?

Key vocabulary

- Satire
- Parody
- Reversal

- experiment in my own compositions with using satire to comment on or critique an aspect of society
- explore and reflect on the purpose of satire.

What is satire?

Satire is when we blend humour with criticism. Joseph Hall (satirist) best described satire in the following way:

> The Satyre should be like the Porcupine,
> That shoots sharpe quils out in each angry line,
> And wounds the blushing cheeke, and fiery eye,
> Of him that heares, and readeth guiltily.

4.12.1 Warm-up with a partner!

Comedy is 'traditionally the weapon of the powerless against the powerful.' (Molly Ivins)

How can you use comedy to argue a point?

Discuss your response to this question with a partner.

4.12.2 Reading, viewing and listening to texts

Look at these cartoon posters.

Choose one cartoon and write a response to the following questions.

A laugh a minute

1. What is the message of this cartoon? Is it effective? Why or why not?

2 List the comedic conventions used in these cartoons.

3 Based on these cartoons and your own knowledge, explain what satire is. Use your list above to help you create your own definition.

4 Compare your definition with a partner's. Then have a whole class discussion, sharing the similarities of each other's definitions. Can you create a class definition?

Often, satirical texts use humour, irony and wit to **ridicule** their subject, to comment on or criticise society. **Satire** will involve some sort of general criticism of humanity or an aspect of human nature, or specific criticism of an individual or group. Satirists do this to see some sort of change and to ultimately improve humanity.

At the root of any good satire is a voice advocating for change.

To be effective, satire cannot *tell* the audience that someone is wrong or that change needs to happen. It has to show them. Due to this, some satire can be **implicit** and will assume that its audience will understand its critique, that they'll 'get the joke'.

VOCABULARY

Satire
noun: the use of irony, sarcasm, ridicule or the like, to expose, denounce or deride the folly or corruption of institutions, people or social structures.

Ridicule
verb: make fun of; to mock.

Implicit
adjective: something that is suggested rather than directly expressed.

4.12.3 Reading, viewing and listening to texts

One of the best ways to learn about satire is to look at cartoons. For each cartoon, explain what the subject of the satire is and what is the **purpose** or **message**.

Nick Anderson

1 What is the subject of the satire?

2 What is the purpose of each of these cartoons?

3 What is the message of these cartoons and how are you positioned to respond?

What are the common codes and conventions of satire?

Satire employs a range of codes and conventions. In this section, you are going to understand what these are and how to identify them. You will explore when best to use these satirical tools. The main conventions used in satire are exaggeration, incongruity, parody and reversal.

Some of these we have looked at already, but let's take a look at how they are used in satire.

Exaggeration	Incongruity	Irony	Reversal
Exaggeration in satire is the act of enlarging or increasing something so that it becomes ridiculous, so that its faults can be clearly seen. Often, exaggeration is employed to portray something that is unimportant as very important, which highlights its triviality.	As we learned in Chapter 10, incongruity presents things that are out of place or are discordant with something else. Satirists use incongruity to intentionally create this surprise and amusement in their audience.	As we have already learned, irony is when something happens that is the opposite of what was expected. Satire uses the three types of irony: verbal irony, situational irony and dramatic irony. Verbal irony is when what is said is different from what is meant; situational irony occurs when what is expected to happen is the opposite of what actually happens; and dramatic irony arises when the audience knows more information than the characters are aware of.	Reversal is a tool for the satirist to alter the usual order of events or the traditional hierarchical order to make a point. For example, one might serve dessert before the main dish, or the personal assistant might tell the company president what to do. This subverts the 'norm', which prompts the audience to question our assumptions and expectations.

4.12.4 Understanding and responding to texts A

For each of the above conventions, come up with an example from a text.

Convention		Example
Exaggeration	=	____________________
Incongruity	=	____________________
Irony	=	____________________
Reversal	=	____________________

How can satire expose flaws and challenge ideas?

Let's now turn to another example of satire. Mark Twain (1835–1910), an American writer, is well-known for his comical and satirical writing. He wrote many texts that expose flaws and challenge ideas. We are going to read an extract from his second published book, *Roughing It*, which is a semi-autographical collection of stories that were inspired by his travels through the 'Wild West' from 1861 to 1866.

In the beginning of the story, we learn that the protagonist decides to go on a journey to Nevada and he tells everyone that he is doing this to serve as the 'Secretary for the Governor of the Territory'. This is just a sham. He really wants to take advantage of his position to make money. Twain views his journey to the West as an adventure, a way to 'get rich quick', and is initially quite optimistic about it. However, the adventure was not easy (hence the title) and his many attempts to earn money failed.

CONTEXT

The 'Wild West' refers to the expansive area of the growing United States in the 1800s, west of the Mississippi River and traversing to the Pacific Coast. In the 1800s, many people travelled to the West hoping to find adventure, opportunity or a new life.

4.12.5 Reading, viewing and listening to texts

In this extract, we will see that Twain uses mishaps and mistakes to show why he cannot achieve his goals. Much of the satire and humour comes from this.

Roughing It

By Mark Twain

Chapter 42
What to do next?

It was a **momentous** question. I had gone out into the world to **shift** for myself, at the age of thirteen (for my father had endorsed for friends; and although he left us a sumptuous legacy of pride in his fine Virginian stock and its national distinction, I presently found that I could not live on that alone without occasional bread to wash it down with). I had gained a livelihood in various **vocations**, but had not dazzled anybody with my successes; still the list was before me, and the amplest liberty in the matter of choosing, provided I wanted to work – which I did not, after being so wealthy.

I had once been a grocery clerk, for one day, but had consumed so much sugar in that time that I was relieved from further duty by the **proprietor**; said he wanted me outside, so that he could have my custom. I had studied law an entire week, and then given it up because it was so **prosy** and tiresome. I had engaged briefly in the study of blacksmithing, but wasted so much time trying to fix the **bellows** so that it would blow itself, that the master turned me adrift in disgrace, and told me I would come to no good. I had been a bookseller's clerk for awhile,

CONTEXT

After his father's death, the narrator must start out on his own. We learn about a series of jobs he has tried. Twain uses the word 'shift' here, which he is using to suggest work.

IDENTIFY

In this paragraph, Twain exaggerates the narrator's experience through words, like 'momentous'.

PAUSE

Pause here. Discuss with a partner your assumptions about the sort of person the narrator is.

VOCABULARY

Prosy
adjective: dull

but the customers bothered me so much I could not read with any comfort, and so the proprietor gave me a **furlough** and forgot to put a limit to it. I had clerked in a drug store part of a summer, but my prescriptions were unlucky, and we appeared to sell more stomach pumps than soda water. So I had to go.

I had made of myself a tolerable printer, under the impression that I would be another Franklin some day, but somehow had missed the connection thus far. There was no **berth** open in the Esmeralda Union, and besides I had always been such a slow **compositor** that I looked with envy upon the achievements of apprentices of two years' standing; and when I took a 'take,' **foremen** were in the habit of suggesting that it would be wanted 'some time during the year.'

I was a good average St. Louis and New Orleans pilot and by no means ashamed of my abilities in that line; wages were two hundred and fifty dollars a month and no board to pay, and I did long to stand behind a wheel again and never roam any more – but I had been making such an ass of myself lately in **grandiloquent** letters home about my blind lead and my European excursion that I did what many and many a poor disappointed miner had done before; said 'It is all over with me now, and I will never go back home to be pitied – and snubbed.' I had been a private secretary, a silver miner and a silver mill operative, and amounted to less than nothing in each, and now –

What to do next?

IDENTIFY

In Unit 1 we learned about word connotations. Identify the words that have connotative (emotional) meanings.

CONTEXT

In paragraphs 3 and 4, Twain creates **irony**. We understand the reason for why the narrator was fired, but he does not. The irony is created when we understand that this behaviour is not appropriate but the narrator is oblivious to this.

CONTEXT

A pilot is a mariner who can navigate ships through dangerous or busy waterways. Twain was a river-boat pilot on the Mississippi River for two years before travelling west.

1 Look up these words and write down their definitions.

Vocation = ______

Proprietor = ______

Bellows = ______

Furlough = ______

Berth = ______

Compositor = ______

Foreman = ______

Grandiloquent = ______

2 Explain the protagonist's attitude to work. Outline why he had this attitude.

4.12.6 Understanding and responding to texts A

Roughing It is a critical commentary on various aspects of society and culture during the 1800s in America, like wealth, social class and pretention. Twain employs reversal, exaggeration and irony to create the character of the protagonist and highlight the flaws in cultural attitudes.

Work through the following questions to help you identify and explain these conventions of satire.

1 Twain uses incongruity in his characterisation of the narrator. The narrator tells us of his situation:

> '... although [my father] left us a sumptuous legacy of pride in his fine Virginian stock and its national distinction, I presently found that I could not live on that alone without occasional bread to wash it down with.'

a We learn that he comes from a wealthy and respected family. This causes us to have certain expectations about the narrator and his knowledge and abilities. Outline what your assumptions were.

b But we discover that Twain's narrator is naïve and out of place in these environments. Explain how Twain uses incongruity to enhance the characterisation of the narrator.

2 In the beginning of the extract, the narrator reflects:

> 'It was a momentous question. I had gone out into the world to shift for myself, at the age of thirteen ... I had gained a livelihood in various vocations, but had not dazzled anybody with my successes.'

Here, we can see that Twain uses exaggeration through his word choice, 'momentous' and 'dazzled'. The innocence of the narrator is exaggerated to create humour.

a Make a list of other examples of exaggeration.

b Choose an example of exaggeration and explain how it creates comedy.

3 In paragraphs 3 and 4, the narrator outlines the jobs that he attempted and how he was unsuccessful, which creates dramatic irony. For example, when he was a grocery clerk (for one day!) he had 'consumed so much sugar in that time' that he was fired.

a What do you think Twain is suggesting about the narrator?

b Which example of irony in paragraphs 3 and 4 do you think is the most effective?

c How does the use of irony help Twain to create the character of his narrator?

d Explain what you think Twain is satirising.

4 Let's consider our inquiry question: How can satire expose flaws and challenge ideas? Earlier in the chapter, we learned that satirical texts ridicule their subject to comment on or criticise society. Satirists do this to see some sort of change and to ultimately improve humanity. Write a paragraph explaining how Twain's satire does this. Use quotations and refer to exaggeration, reversal and irony.

How can I use satire to make changes in society?

4.12.7 Expressing ideas and composing texts A

We have learned about satire and have looked at some different satirical texts that create a critical commentary on various aspects of society and culture. We have learned about the codes and conventions that satirical texts use to ridicule and create humour.

Think of a social or cultural attitude that you would like to comment on or criticise, that you think needs to change.

Write the opening of a satirical text in which you ridicule this attitude. Include conventions like exaggeration, incongruity, reversal and irony.

Make sure you have a clear purpose, audience and effect that you want to create.

4.12.8 Chapter reflection

1 I enjoy/do not enjoy (circle one) satire because ...

2 In this chapter, the activity that I liked the most was ______ because ...

3 What is the overall aim of satire?

4 Why might someone choose to create a satirical text to present their perspective? What makes satire an effective way to present your opinion?

5 Let's return to the unit inquiry question: ***What role does comedy play in our lives?*** Based on what you have learned in this chapter, do you think satire serves an important part in our lives?

Unit 4: **Summative assessment**

The summative assessment options below provide opportunities to demonstrate your achievement of the following outcomes and focus areas:

Outcome	EN5-RVL-01 Reading, viewing and listening to texts	EN5-URA-01 Understanding and responding to texts A	EN5-URB-01 Understanding and responding to texts B	EN4-URC-01 Understanding and responding to texts C	EN5-ECA-01 Expressing ideas and composing texts A
	Reading, viewing and listening for meaning	Code and convention	Perspective and context	Genre	Representing Speaking Word-level language

Option 1: Podcast

A Laugh a Minute is a humorous and thought-provoking podcast that dives into the nature of comedy and its importance in our daily lives. Hosted by a witty and charismatic comedian, the show weaves together funny observations and insightful discussions to discuss the multifaceted nature of comedy.

You are to create an episode for this podcast. Your podcast's topic is to investigate the quote: 'Laughter is bodily exercise, precious to health' (Aristotle). Your episode should focus on the role comedy plays in our lives in terms of the benefits of laughter and comedy for our mental health and well-being.

Be guided by the following questions to plan, write and produce your podcast.

- What are the benefits of laughing?
- How is comedy good for us? Explore the role that comedy can play in our lives.
- How can you analyse the ways in which comedic codes and conventions in texts create humour?
- How can you make vocabulary choices that enhance your writing (e.g. the language of comedy like exaggeration, irony, incongruity etc.) and shape meaning through connotation?
- In what ways can you speak with intonation, emphasis, volume, pace and timing to engage your audience?
- What music and/or sound clips can you use to make your podcast engaging?

Option 2: Narrated visual presentation

'Laughter is timeless.' – Walt Disney

In this unit, one of the big ideas about comedy is its timeless nature and how the genre has changed over the last 2000 years. You are to create a multimodal presentation that explores the question: To what extent is comedy timeless?

You are to create a visual representation tool with a voice over. Choose two of the texts examined in this unit, one older text and one newer. Compose a multimodal presentation that presents your opinion on whether comedy withstands the test of time. Does comedy remain relevant, relatable and humorous across generations? And, if so, what role does comedy play in our lives?

You might consider delving into ...

- iconic comedians, sketches, sitcoms or stand-up performances that have left a lasting impact
- the world of the classic and contemporary comedy genre, making connections between past and present comedy
- the subjective nature of comedy, investigating the codes and conventions that allow comedy to transcend time.

Be guided by the following questions to plan and create your presentation.

- What is your position on the topic?
- How has the comedy genre changed?
- How can you analyse the ways in which comedic codes and conventions in texts create humour?
- How can you make vocabulary choices that enhance your writing (e.g. the language of comedy like exaggeration, irony, incongruity etc.) and shape meaning through connotation?
- In what ways can you speak with intonation, emphasis, volume, pace and timing to engage your audience?
- What images, music and/or sound clips can you use to make your presentation effective?

Option 3: Video essay

You are to demonstrate your understanding of satire through a video essay that responds to the prompt: 'Against the assault of laughter, nothing can stand' (Mark Twain). Your video essay should explore the purpose and impact of satire, highlighting its role in society and our daily lives.

A video essay combines audio, visuals, text and voice to develop an argument or explore a topic. Choose one satirical text from this unit and another of your own choosing. Your response should be an organised and coherent argument on the topic that presents your knowledge and understanding of satire.

Be guided by the following questions to plan, write and produce your video essay.

- What are the common codes and conventions of satire?
- How can satire expose flaws and challenge ideas?
- What texts from this unit can you use to help illustrate your ideas?

- How can you analyse the ways in which comedic codes and conventions in texts create satire?
- How can you make vocabulary choices that enhance your writing (e.g. the technical language of satire exaggeration, irony, incongruity etc.) and shape meaning through connotation?
- In what ways can you speak with intonation, emphasis, volume, pace and timing to engage your audience?
- What images, text, music and/or sound clips can you use to make your podcast engaging?

Assessment as learning: self-assessment

Does my multimodal text ...

- ☐ present an opinion on the topic and explore the role comedy plays?
- ☐ analyse how comedic codes and conventions create comedy?
- ☐ use a range of modes (visual, written, aural etc.)?
- ☐ have a spoken element with engaging use of intonation, emphasis, volume, pace and timing?
- ☐ make vocabulary choices that enhance my writing?

What are two strengths of my response?

____

____

What area/s of my response do I need to refine further?

____

____

ACKNOWLEDGEMENTS

Insight Publications thanks the authors, Emma Wynne-Jones and Bronwyn Ralphs, for all their work on *English for NSW, Year 9, Stage 5*.

Insight Publications is also grateful to the following individuals and organisations for permission to reproduce copyright material.

Texts: NESA website: English K-10 Syllabus © NSW Education Standards Authority for and on behalf of the Crown in right of the State of New South Wales, 2012; Extract: Jenish Pandya, 'What does being an Australian mean to you?' by Harita Mehta, SBS Hindi, 25 January 2018; Extract: *The Hate Race* by Maxine Beneba Clarke, Hachette Australia Books 2022; Poem: 'We Real Cool The pool players Seven at the golden shovel.' by Gwendolyn Brooks, Reprinted by Consent of Brooks Permissions; 'Fish Cheeks' by Amy Tan © 1987 by Amy Tan. First appeared in Seventeen Magazine. Reprinted by permission of the author and the Sandra Dijkstra Literary Agency.; 'How Kobe Bryant Willed Himself to Greatness' by Colin Robertson, Willpowered.com; Poem: 'Every day the planet burns a little more' by Brian Bilston ©Brian Bilston, Jo Unwin Literary Agency; Graphic novel extract: *Che Guevara A Manga Biography* by Chie Shimano and Kiyoshi Konno, Penguin Australia and Chie Shimano; Extract: Fisola Kenny-Akinnuoye; Poem: 'An Ode We Owe' by Amanda Gorman © Amanda Gorman; Poem: 'For the Children' by Gary Snyder, New Directions Publishing © Gary Snyder; Poem: 'Climate emergency' by Tess Rooney; Poem: 'Attack' by Siegfried Sassoon, The Barbara Levy Agency; Extract: 'United Nations Charter' by United Nations; Extract: '16th birthday speech to the United Nations' by Malala Yousafzai, Malala Yousafzai and Malala.org; 'The Scholarship Jacket' by Marta Salinas, Bilingual Press and Marta Salinas; Poem: 'When the Last Human Being' by Francis Duggan; ; Extract: THE HUNGER GAMES by Suzanne Collins, Copyright © 2008 by Suzanne Collins, Reprinted by permission of Scholastic Inc.; Extract: *The Return of the King* by JRR Tolkien, HarperCollins UK; Extract: *The Gospel of Loki* by Joanne Harris, Simon & Schuster USA; Extract: *Wyrd Sisters* by Terry Pratchett, Penguin Random House UK 'What Heroes Do' by Heather Kuehl, Flash Fiction Online; Extract: *My Life is a Wedgie* by Gretel Killeen, Penguin Books Australia; Extract:'The Play That Goes Wrong®' and 'The One-Act Play That Goes Wrong' by Henry Lewis, Jonathan Sayer and Henry Shields, © Bloomsbury Publishing Pty 2023.

Images: Poster: 'Man your eskys', australiaday.org.au; Cover image: *Che Guevara A Manga Biography* by Chie Shimano and Kiyoshi Konno, Penguin Australia and Chie Shimano; Cover image: *Please Don't Paint Our Planet Pink!* by Gregg Kleiner, Cloudburst Creative!; Cover image: *Something New Under the Sun* by Alexandra Kleeman, Random House Global ; Cover image: *Loki Where mischief lies* by Mackenzi Lee, Disney Publishing Group; Aunty Dr Matilda House-Williams, NAIDOC.org; Cartoon: 'When a man does not look his best', Punch Magazine and Topfoto UK; Cover image: *Walt Disney Comic*, Disney Publishing Group; Cover image: 'The One-Act Play that Goes Wrong' by Henry Lewis, Jonathan Sayer and Henry Shields, © Bloomsbury Publishing Pty 2023; Cartoon: 'Facebook', ©Nick Anderson, Tribune Content Agency. The following images from Alamy: Sauron, Lady Macbeth. Fred Hollows, Eddie Mabo, Eat mor chikin, Spring is here, What kind of cows does oat milk come from?; The following images from Wikimedia Commons: Cathy Freeman, Johnathan Thurston, Ian Frazer, Rosie Batty, Tim Costello. Additional images from Shutterstock.

Notes

Notes

Notes